COPYCAT RECIPES

+130 Step-by-Step Recipes to cook the most famous restaurant dishes at home, save money and dramatically improve your cooking skills.

Emma Dennis

Table of Contents

Chapter 3 Cracker Barrel™ Favorites 61

Chapter 4 Olive Garden™ Favorites 85

Chapter 5 P.F. Chang's™ Favorites 113

Chapter 7 Red Lobster™ Favorites 157

Chapter 8 Panera Bread™ Favorites 188

and are the owned by the owners themselves, not affiliated
with this document.

Introduction

Congratulations on purchasing *Copycat Recipes,* and thank you for doing so. You will be surprised how delicious home cooking is when you can prepare a delicious plate of food, and wonder who you need to "tip" for the excellent flavor. Oh, that is right, you cooked it!

The following chapters will discuss delicious recipes you have not been able to enjoy previously unless you dined out or chose deliveries exorbitantly priced.

Top Benefits Of Preparing Copycat Recipes:

Improvement of your cooking skills will surface as you discover each of the many ways to prepare the delicious menus in your cookbook.

- Save Money

- Save Time

- Consume Healthier Ingredients

- Avoid Food Allergies

- Portion Control

- Benefits Your Health

- Elimination Of Ingredients That May Cause Allergies

- Genuine Preparation Methods Provided In Your Kitchen

- Improved Eating Habits Are Possible

- Greater Control of Your Diet

Consider adding a high-quality set of scales to your inventory to ensure your delicious recipes are adequately measured. There is nothing more disappointing than to finish roasting or baking your meal to have it ruined! Look for these guidelines:

- *Seek A Conversion Button:* You need to know how to convert measurements into grams since not all recipes have them listed. The grams keep the system in complete harmony.
- *Check For The Tare Function:* When you set a bowl on the scale, the feature will allow you to reset the weight back to zero (0).
- *Have A Removable Plate:* Keep the germs off of the scale by removing the plate. Be sure it will come off (before purchasing) to eliminate any bacterial buildup.

These are a few more vital tools you will need to compete with the pro's guidelines:

- *Wire cooling racks* are useful in cooling bread, muffins, and many other dishes.

- *Cutting boards* are used during many phases of prep. Consider having different colored heavy-duty plastic boards for each type of food item to help prevent cross-contamination.

- *Measuring cups* are needed for liquid and dry ingredients.

- *Measuring spoons* are essential for a successful dish. If you do a lot of baking and cooking, consider a magnetic set, so the spoon is never lost, and they will also fit into spice jars.

- *Sifter:* Purchase a good sifter for under $10, and you will be ensured a more accurate measurement for your baking needs.

- *Whisks* can be purchased in different sizes and are used in many recipes.

- *Saucepans:* Boiling vegetables and pasta will require a pan that's easily maneuvered when filled. Start with a 4-quart pan, whether you are cooking for one or four.

- *Non-Stick Frying Pan:* A non-stick pan is vital if you want to deliver a delicious and eye-appealing egg meal as the big restaurants provide. You can also sauté veggies, sear meats, and prepare delicious sauces. Have two sizes on hand, so you can make different steps of the recipes (save time too).

- *Sheet Pans:* A baking tray can quickly become one of the most used items in the kitchen as you prepare your delicious copycat recipes. You can bake meat, roast veggies, toast nuts, and make trays of delicious sweets.

You will also want to have a dampened tea towel, plastic wrap, and a package of parchment baking paper. This is a fairly accurate list of the accessories you will need to begin your new cooking adventure.

Let's Get Started!

Chapter 1

Applebees™ Favorites

Breakfast

Brunch Bourbon Street Steak

Servings Provided: 4
Total Prep & Cook Time: 35 Minutes

Ingredients:

- Steak sauce - ex. A1™ (.5 cup)
- Honey (1 tbsp.)
- Bourbon whiskey (.25 cup)
- Prepared mustard (2 tsp.)
- Cajun spices (1 tsp.)
- Steak - chuck/round/rib (40 oz.)

Preparation Directions:

1. Combine each of the fixings in a zipper-type bag. Add the steaks and marinate them for two hours to overnight.
2. Cooking Time: Warm the grill in advance using the med-high temperature setting.
3. Grill them for 12-15 minutes until they are as you like them. They are fantastic for dinner also.

Brunch Quesadillas

Servings Provided: 1
Total Prep & Cook Time: 25 Minutes

Ingredients:

- Bacon (2 slices)
- Colby jack cheese (.25 cup)
- Butter (2 tsp.)
- Tortillas (2)
- Pico de Gallo (1 tbsp.)
  To Garnish:
- Sour cream (1 tbsp.)
- Guacamole (1 tbsp.)
- Picante sauce (1 tbsp.)

Preparation Directions:

1. Slice the bacon into ½-inch pieces and shred the cheese.
2. Cook the bacon until it's crispy - not hard, and set it aside on towels to drain.
3. Add butter to one side of the shell and place it on a heated pan.
4. Garnish using two tablespoons of bacon over the shell and add the fixings.

5. Add the second shell with the butter side upwards.
6. Cook about 1-2 minutes to heat the fixings, flip, and finish the process.
7. Serve when it is hot - not browned. Enjoy it with salsa, sour cream, or your favorite sauces.

Sage Chicken Tender Platter

Servings Provided: 4
Total Prep & Cook Time: 30 Minutes

Ingredients:

- Buttermilk (.5 cup)
- Hot pepper sauce (.25 tsp.)
- Salt (.75 tsp.)
- Black pepper ⅛ tsp.)
- Chicken tenderloins (1 lb.)
- Panko breadcrumbs (1 cup)
- Freshly minced sage (2-3 tbsp.)
- Optional: Ranch salad dressing
- Oil for Frying: As needed

Preparation Directions:

1. Whisk the buttermilk, pepper, pepper sauce, and salt. Add the chicken and marinate it for about 15 minutes.
2. Add the breadcrumbs to a shallow container with the sage.
3. Dredge the tenderloins through the breadcrumbs and place them into the skillet.

4. Cook the chicken in a deep skillet (365° Fahrenheit) in one inch of oil.
5. Fry them for two to three minutes per side until browned to your liking.
6. Drain on paper towels and dust with salt as desired.
7. Serve with the dressing.

Lunch

Asian Chicken Salad With Dressing

Servings Provided: 4
Total Prep & Cook Time: 30-35 Minutes

Ingredients:

The Chicken:
- Chicken (1 lb. - bite-size pieces)
- Panko breadcrumbs (1.5 cups)
- Honey (2 tbsp.)

The Salad:
- Napa cabbage (4 cups)
- Romaine lettuce (4 cups)
- Red cabbage (.5 cup)
- Dry chow mein noodles (1 cup)
- Mandarin oranges (4 peeled and slices pulled apart)
- Slivered almonds (.5 cup)
- Chopped green onions (.33 cup)

The Dressing:
- Sugar (1 tsp.)
- Greek yogurt - plain (.5 cup)

- Dijon-style mustard (1 tbsp.)
- Soy sauce (1.5 tsp.)
- Rice wine vinegar (.33 cup)
- Honey (2 tbsp.)
- Toasted sesame oil (.5 tsp. or more to your liking)
- Olive oil (2-3 tbsp.)

Preparation Directions:

1. Set the oven temperature at 375° Fahrenheit. Spritz a baking tray using a cooking oil spray.
2. Pour the breadcrumbs in a shallow dish. Cut the skin and bones from the chicken and dice. Toss it in with the honey, and dip each chicken piece into the breadcrumbs.
3. Set a timer to bake the chicken until thoroughly cooked (20 min.).
4. Rinse and chop the lettuce and cabbage. Discard the peel from the oranges.
5. Whisk the yogurt and vinegar, soy sauce, mustard, honey, sugar, sesame oil, and olive oil until smooth.
6. Toss the lettuce, Napa, and red cabbage. Prepare using four salad bowls, adding the noodles, almonds, and green onions. Mix in the whole orange (slices pulled apart).
7. Add the dressing and serve.

French Onion Soup

Total Preparation & Cook Time: 1 ¾ Hours
Servings Provided: 8

Ingredients:
- Butter (2 tbsp.)
- Vegetable oil (2 tbsp.)
- White onions (6-7 large/10 cups)
- Salt (1 tsp.)
- Garlic (1.5 tsp.)
- Beef broth (10 cups)
- Beef base - ex. Better Than Bouillon (1 tbsp.)
- Black pepper (1 tsp.)
- Firm bread (8 slices)
- Provolone cheese (8 slices/8 tbsp.)
- Parmesan cheese (8 tsp. grated)
- Also Needed: 8 oven-proof bowls

Preparation Directions:

1. Use the medium temperature setting to melt the butter and oil in a stockpot. Slice the onions and sauté with salt until they're browned (½ hour). Stir them often. Once they are thoroughly caramelized, mince and add in the garlic, and sauté them until fragrant (2 min.).
2. Pour in the broth, pepper, and beef base. Adjust salt as desired and simmer using the low-temperature setting for 30-45 minutes.
3. Warm the oven on the broil function. Ladle the soup into the bowls, with one teaspoon of the parmesan and provolone cheese. Broil them until browned and serve.

Dinner

Mexican Fiesta Lime Chicken

Servings Provided: 4
Total Prep & Cook Time: 30 Minutes

Ingredients:

- Chicken breasts (4 boneless & skinless)
- Olive oil (2 tbsp.)
- Black pepper and seasoning salt - ex. Lawry's (as desired)
- Ranch Dressing (.25 cup)
- Greek yogurt (.25 cup)
- Lime juice (1 tbsp.)
- Fresh cilantro (.25 cup)
- Garlic (1 clove)
- Colby - Monterey Jack Cheese (4 slices)
- To Garnish: Pico de Gallo (see below) - cilantro - tortilla strips
- To Serve: Mexican rice

Preparation Directions:

1. Chop the cilantro and set it aside. Warm the grill at 400° Fahrenheit.
2. Spritz each piece of chicken with oil, pepper, and salt as desired.
3. Arrange the chicken pieces on the grill. Let them sizzle for ten minutes on each side. You want the chicken to be thoroughly cooked - no longer be pink inside.
4. Meanwhile, prepare the dressing in a blender mixing the yogurt, ranch, juice of the lime, garlic, and cilantro until it's creamy.
5. Scoop one tablespoon of the ranch mix on top of each breast and top it off with cheese. Place it on the grill to melt the cheese.
6. Serve with the toppings as desired with a side of rice to your liking.

Pico De Gallo Delight

Servings Provided: 6
Total Prep & Cook Time: 20 Minutes (+) rest time

Ingredients:

- Onion (1 cup)
- Jalapenos (2 tbsp.)
- Large tomatoes (3)
- Black pepper (.5 tsp.)
- Fresh cilantro (.5 cup)
- Salt (2 tsp.)
- Garlic powder (.5 tsp.)
- White vinegar (1 tbsp.)
- Olive oil (1 tbsp.)

Preparation Directions:

1. Dice the jalapenos, onion, and tomatoes. Toss each of the fixings in a large mixing container.
2. Let it rest in a closed container for a minimum of six hours (even better overnight).

Sides

Oriental Dressing

Servings Provided: 12 Tablespoons
Total Prep & Cook Time: 10 Minutes

Ingredients:

- Honey (3 tbsp.)
- Dijon mustard ex. Grey Poupon (1 tsp.)
- Rice vinegar (1.5 tbsp.)
- Hellmann's Mayonnaise (.25 cup)
- Sesame oil (.125 tsp.)

Preparation Directions:

1. Mix each of the fixings in a mixing container.
2. Place a lid or plastic wrap on it and store it in the fridge.

Dessert

Apple Chimi cheesecake

Servings Provided: 1
Total Prep & Cook Time: 23-25 Minutes

Ingredients:

- Gala apple (1)
- Brown sugar (.25 cup)
- Butter (1 tbsp.)
- Unchilled cream cheese (8 oz.)
- Vanilla (1 tsp.)
- White sugar (.25 cup)
- Floured tortilla (1 burrito-sized)

    To Serve
- Sugar-cinnamon mixture
- Vanilla ice cream
- Caramel sauce

Preparation Directions:

1. Chop the apple and toss it into a small pot (medium temp) with the butter and brown sugar. Simmer the

mixture, stirring continuously until the apples are softened. Wait for it to cool.

2. Blend the cream cheese, vanilla, and white sugar using a hand mixer until it's smooth.
3. Fold in the apple mixture. Spread butter and rub the cinnamon and sugar over one side of the tortilla.
4. Scoop the cheesecake mixture into the center (of the opposite side) of the tortilla. Tuck in the sides and roll it like a burrito.
5. Place it into a skillet to cook using the medium temperature setting until it's crispy, flipping as needed to cook it evenly.
6. Slice it in half. Serve as desired with a scoop of ice cream and a drizzle of caramel sauce.

Maple Walnut Blondie

Servings Provided: 9
Total Prep & Cook Time: 40 Minutes

Ingredients:

- Brown sugar (1 cup - packed)
- Salt (.125 tsp.)
- Baking powder (.5 tsp.)
- Flour - All-purpose (1 cup)
- Baking soda (.125 tsp.)
- Chopped walnuts (.25 cup)
- Melted butter (.33 cup)
- Large egg (1)
- Vanilla extract (1 tbsp.)
- White chocolate chips (.5 cup)

  The Sauce
- Softened butter (.25 cup)
- Powdered sugar (.25 cup)
- Softened cream cheese (2 tbsp./1 oz.)
- Maple syrup (1 tbsp.)
- Also Needed: An 8 by 8-inch pan

Preparation Directions:

1. Set the oven to reach 350° Fahrenheit. Prepare the pan using a layer of foil and misting of a cooking oil spray.
2. Whisk and add the baking powder and soda, flour, salt, and walnuts in a mixing dish.
3. In a separate container, mix the brown sugar, softened butter, vanilla, and egg using an electric mixer. Gradually, fold in the flour mixture and chocolate chips, and add to the pan to bake for 20 to 25 minutes.
4. Combine the cream cheese, maple syrup, butter, and powdered sugar. Blend with a mixer until the mixture until it's creamy smooth.
5. Serve the treat warm with a portion of ice cream and tasty sauce.

Triple Chocolate Meltdown

Servings Provided: 2
Total Prep & Cook Time: 20 Minutes

Ingredients:

The Cake:
- Semisweet chocolate (4 oz.)
- Butter (4 oz.)
- Large eggs (2) + Egg yolks (2 large)
- All-purpose flour (2 tbsp.)
- Salt (.25 tsp.)

The Drizzle:
- White chocolate (4 oz.)
- Semisweet chocolate (4 oz.)
- Vegetable shortening (2 tsp.)
- Vanilla ice cream (2 cups)
- Also Needed: 4 small ramekins (6 oz.)

Preparation Directions:

1. Warm the oven to 400° Fahrenheit.
2. Prepare the ramekins with butter and a sprinkling of sugar.

3. Add water to double water to melt the butter and chocolate chips (4 oz each). Whisk it intermittently until it's creamy.
4. Whisk the eggs and ¼ cup of sugar until combined.
5. Pour the chocolate mixture into the eggs - quickly stir. Mix in the salt and flour until just combined.
6. Pour the batter into the ramekins and place them on a baking tray.
7. Set the timer for eight minutes (the middle will be soft).
8. Invert each of the cakes onto a serving dish (after about 30 sec.).
9. Make the toppings in individual dishes. Add one teaspoon of shortening to each bowl. Melt it using 15- second increments in the microwave. Stir until mixed.
10. Drizzle the white and chocolate over the cake to serve.

Chapter 2

Cheesecake Factory™ Favorites

Breakfast & Brunch

Avocado Egg Rolls

Servings Provided: 8 rolls
Total Prep & Cook Time: 20-25 Minutes

Ingredients:

- Juice of 1 lime
- Avocados (3)
- Roma tomato (1)
- Red onion (.25 cup)
- Cilantro leaves (2 tbsp.)
- Black pepper and kosher salt (as desired)
- Egg roll wrappers (8)
- Vegetable oil (1 cup)

The Sauce
- Fresh cilantro leaves (.75 cup - loosely packed)
- Sour cream (.33 cup)
- Optional: Jalapeno (1/seeded to your taste)
- Mayonnaise (2 tbsp.)
- Clove of garlic (1)
- Juice of 1 lime
- Black pepper & Kosher salt (as desired)

Preparation Directions:

1. Dice the onion, tomato, and cilantro. Slice the avocado in half, peel, and remove the seeds.
2. Use a food processor to prepare the dipping sauce by combining the garlic, pepper, salt, cilantro, mayo, jalapeno, sour cream, and lime juice. Set the bowl aside.
3. Warm the oil in a large skillet using the med-high temperature setting.
4. Mash the avocados. Fold in the tomato, onion, lime juice, cilantro, salt, and pepper to your liking.
5. Scoop the avocado mixture in the middle of each wrapper. Tightly roll it over the filling, folding in the sides. Rub the edges of the wrapper with water, pressing to seal.
6. Arrange the rolls to the skillet and cook them until crispy as desired (2-3 min.). Transfer them onto a platter lined with paper towels.
7. Serve and enjoy them with the dipping sauce.

Creme Brulee French Toast

Servings Provided: 8/1-inch slices
Total Prep & Cook Time: 25-30 Minutes

Ingredients:

- Loaf of Brioche (1.5 lb. - day old is best)
- Whole large eggs (5) + Egg yolk (1)
- Half & Half (1.25 cups)
- Vanilla (1 tbsp.)
- Sugar (2 tbsp.)
- For Cooking: Butter

    The Syrup:
- Heavy cream (1 cup)
- Butter (.5 cup)
- Brown sugar (.5 cup)
- Maple extract (.25 tsp.)
- Salt (1 dash)
- Vanilla (.5 tsp.)

Preparation Directions:

1. Slice the bread into eight one-inch slices.

2. Whisk all of the eggs, vanilla, sugar, and Half & Half. Dip the slices of bread in the mixture and let it absorb the egg mixture for about one minute. Flip it over to let the second side soak. Allow the excess egg mixture to drip off into a mixing bowl.
3. Warm a skillet or griddle up to 350° Fahrenheit. Melt butter in the skillet. Arrange the toast pieces in the pan and cook until lightly browned on the first side. As the french toast is cooking, sprinkle it using sugar on the uncooked side. Turn them over and finish cooking until golden and sugar is caramelized. Serve with the delicious syrup.
4. Make the syrup. Pour the cream, butter, and brown sugar in a saucepan using the medium temperature setting. Once it's boiling, cook for about one minute. Transfer the saucepan to a cool burner and add a dash of salt, maple extract, and vanilla.

Fish & Chips

Servings Provided: 4
Total Prep & Cook Time: 30 Minutes

Ingredients:

- Frozen steak fries (4 cups)
- Salmon fillets (4/6 oz. each)
- Prepared horseradish (1-2 tbsp.)
- Parmesan cheese (1 tbsp. - grated)
- Worcestershire sauce (1 tbsp.)
- Salt (.25 tsp.)
- Dijon-style mustard (1 tsp.)
- Panko breadcrumbs (.5 cup)
- Cooking oil spray (as needed)

Preparation Directions:

1. Set the oven to 450° Fahrenheit. Arrange the fries on a baking tray (one layer) and place it on the lowest rack of the oven. Cook the fries until they are as you like them (15-20 min.).
2. Lightly spray a baking tray with a spritz of cooking oil. Arrange the salmon on it and set it aside.
3. Mix the horseradish, Worcestershire sauce, salt, cheese, and mustard. Stir in the breadcrumbs. Press the coating over each of the fillets. Spritz the tops with the oil spray.
4. Sit the tray on the middle rack and set the timer to bake the salmon for about ten minutes. Serve the salmon when it's ready (easily flakes) with the fries.

Huevos Rancheros

Servings Provided: 1
Total Prep & Cook Time: 20 Minutes

Ingredients:

- Tortilla (1)
- Butter (1 tbsp.)
- Shredded cheddar cheese (.5 cup)
- Eggs (3)
- Sour cream (.25 cup)
- Taco sauce (.25 cup)
- Sliced avocado - wedges (¼ of 1)
- Cilantro - minced (1 tbsp.)

Preparation Directions:

1. Warm a sauté pan using the medium-high temperature setting.
2. Add the butter to melt and add a tortilla. Top it off with cheese and the other tortilla.
3. Brown both sides and remove it from the pan and slice it into wedges. Put it on a plate for now.
4. Heat the rest of the butter in the skillet and crack the eggs into the pan. Lower the temperature setting to cook the eggs as desired.

5. Arrange the eggs in the middle of the wedges. Spritz the sauce over the whites of the eggs (not the yolks). Add a scoop of sour cream and the avocado slices with a dusting of cilantro to serve.

Lunch

Beets With Goat Cheese Salad

Servings Provided: 12
Total Prep & Cook Time: 1 ¼ Hours

Ingredients:

- Fresh beets (3 medium/1 lb.)
- Grated orange zest (1 tsp.)
- Orange juice (2 tbsp.)
- White wine vinegar (1 tbsp.)
- Honey (2 tsp.)
- Olive oil (3 tbsp.)
- Dijon-style mustard (1 tsp.)
- Black pepper (.25 tsp.)
- Salt (.5 tsp.)
- Freshly minced tarragon - divided (3 tbsp.)
- Fresh baby spinach (6 oz. pkg.)
- Torn mixed salad greens (4 cups)
- Navel oranges (2 medium)
- Crumbled goat cheese (4 oz.)
- Toasted - chopped walnuts (.5 cup)

Preparation Directions:

1. Warm the oven at 425° Fahrenheit.
2. Scrub beets and trim tops to one inch and wrap them in foil. Place them on a baking tray.
3. Bake the beets for 50-60 minutes or until tender. Remove the foil and cool thoroughly. Peel the beets and cut into wedges.
4. Peel and section the oranges. Whisk the vinegar, oil, orange zest, orange juice, honey, salt, pepper, mustard until blended. Stir in one tablespoon of tarragon. Combine the spinach, salad greens, and rest of the tarragon. Drizzle with vinaigrette and toss gently to coat.
5. Transfer to a platter or divide among 12 salad plates. Top with orange sections and beets; sprinkle with cheese and walnuts. Serve right away.

Bistro Shrimp Pasta

Servings Provided: 2
Total Prep & Cook Time: 15 Minutes

Ingredients:

- Angel hair pasta (4 oz. uncooked)
- Jumbo shrimp (8)
- Fresh asparagus spears (6)
- Olive oil (.25 cup)
- Minced garlic (2 cloves)
- Mushrooms (.5 cup)
- Chicken broth (.5 cup)
- Crushed red pepper flakes (1/8 tsp.)
- Plum tomato (1 small)
- Salt (.25 tsp.)
- Fresh herbs: Oregano, parsley - thyme & basil (1 tbsp. each)
- Parmesan cheese (.25 cup)

Preparation Directions:

1. Cook pasta according to package instructions.
2. Trim the asparagus into two-inch pieces, removing the tips. Devein and peel the shrimp. Sauté the

shrimp and asparagus in oil until shrimp turn pink (3-4 min.).

3. Mince and fold in the garlic and sauté for one minute.
4. Peel and deseed the tomatoes. Slice and fold in the mushrooms, tomato, broth, pepper flakes, and salt. Simmer the mixture with the lid off (2 min.).
5. Dump and drain the pasta into a colander.
6. Fold in the pasta and seasonings with a sprinkle of the cheese.

Chicken Madeira

Servings Provided: 4
Total Prep & Cook Time: 1 ¼ Hours
Ingredients:

For the Chicken:
- Olive oil - divided (5 tbsp.)
- Freshly cracked black pepper & kosher salt (as desired)
- Shredded mozzarella cheese (1 cup)
- Chicken breast fillets (4 skinless)

For the Sauce:
- Olive oil (2 tbsp.)
- Black pepper (.25 tsp.)
- White mushrooms (8 oz.)
- Madeira Wine (3 cups/almost all of the bottle)
- Minced garlic (4 cloves)
- Beef broth (2 cups)
- Cornstarch (2 tbsp. - dissolved in 2 tbsp. of the broth)
- Salted butter (1 tbsp.)

Preparation Directions:

1. The meal is kid-friendly since the alcohol content evaporates during its cooking process.
2. Use a mallet to flatten the chicken (¼-inch thickness). Dust it using the pepper and salt.
3. Heat oil (3 tbsp.) in a large skillet (med-high temp).
4. Arrange the chicken in the pan and fry for three to four minutes per side until they are thoroughly cooked in the center. Place them onto a baking tray and cover to keep them warm.
5. Use the same skillet (unwashed) and add two tablespoons of oil to the pan, heating it until hot. Slice and toss the mushrooms into the pan and sauté for about one to two minutes.
6. Toss in the remainder of the sauce fixings. Stir and wait for it to boil. Adjust the temperature setting to simmer until it has reduced by about ¼ of its original volume and is thickened and browned (20 min.). Pour it into a container to keep warm.
7. Sprinkle the cheese over the chicken in a baking tray. Broil it for three to four minutes until the cheese is melted and browned.
8. Serve pronto with a drizzle of the sauce. Enjoy it with some rice, angel hair pasta, or mashed potatoes!

Creamy Sun-Dried Tomato Fettuccine

Servings Provided: 4
Total Prep & Cook Time: 30 Minutes

Ingredients:

- Dry fettuccine (.75 lb.)
- Reserved pasta water (1 cup)
- Olive oil (2 tbsp.)
- Garlic (5 cloves)
- Sun-dried tomato halves (.5 cup)
- Petite diced tomatoes (14.5 oz. can)
- Tomato paste (1 tbsp.)
- Granulated sugar (2-3 tbsp.)
- Non-fat Greek yogurt - plain (.5 cup)
- Light sour cream (.25 cup)
- Baby spinach (1.5 cups)
- Pepper & salt (as desired)
- Red pepper flakes (to taste)

Preparation Directions:

1. Mince the garlic. Slice the tomatoes into halves and drain. Drain the canned tomatoes also.

2. Add water to a stockpot with one tablespoon of oil. Once boiling, add the fettuccine. Prepare the noodles following the package instructions. Drain and save one cup of the water.
3. In another container, mix the sour cream, and yogurt. Set the bowl aside.
4. Add the rest of the oil (3 tbsp.) to a skillet and warm it using the med-high temperature setting.
5. Once it's hot, mince and add the sun-dried halved tomatoes. Sauté for about two minutes.
6. Lower the temperature to med-low and stir in the diced tomatoes, sugar, and tomato paste. Stir thoroughly.
7. Whisk the sour cream and yogurt until creamy. Warm everything using the med-high setting and simmer for about five to seven minutes.
8. Sprinkle it with pepper and salt. Stir in the spinach and stir until it's wilted, or add it to the cooked pasta. Extinguish the heat. Toss to cover the pasta.
9. Serve it hot with a sprinkle of pepper flakes as desired.

Luau Salad

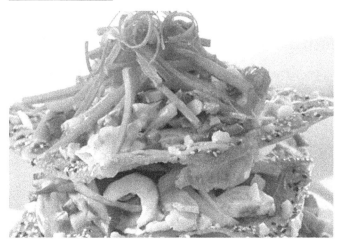

Servings Provided: 6
Total Prep & Cook Time: 45 Minutes

Ingredients:

- Chicken breasts (3)
- Chinese Five Spice Powder (.5 tsp.)
- Red & Yellow bell pepper (1 each)
- Fresh green beans (1.5 cups blanched)
- Fresh mango (1)
- Red onion (1)
- Cucumber slices (1 cup)

  The Dressing:
- Granulated sugar (.25 cup)
- Sesame oil (1 tsp.)
- Rice vinegar (.25 cup)
- Balsamic vinaigrette (.25 cup)
- Kosher salt (1 tsp.)
- Black pepper (.25 tsp.)

  Possible Garnishes:
- Green onions (1 oz. sliced)
- Sweet & Sour Sauce (4 oz.)
- Macadamia nuts (4 oz.)

- Carrots (4 oz.)
- White & Black sesame seeds (2 tsp. each)
- Egg roll wrappers (8 - 6-inches each)

Preparation Directions:

1. Do the prep—grill and slice the chicken into thin strips. Also, slice the peppers into strips. Dice the mango and onion into small pieces. Slice the cucumber and other garnishes to your liking.
2. Toss the chicken using the Five Spice powder.
3. Toss the cucumber slices, mixed greens, peppers, green beans, chicken, mango, onions, pepper, and salt in a jumbo-sized salad bowl.
4. Prepare another container and whisk the vinaigrette, vinegar, sesame oil, and sugar.
5. Spritz the dressing over the salad and gently toss.
6. Smudge a portion of the sweet and sour sauce over each crispy egg roll wrapper to serve.

Pasta Da Vinci

Servings Provided: 6
Total Prep & Cook Time: 45 Minutes

Ingredients:

- Also Needed: Cast-iron skillet
- Penne pasta (1 lb.)
- Chicken breast (1 lb. into 1-inch chunks)
- Butter - divided (4 tbsp.)
- Black pepper (.25 tsp.)
- Kosher salt (.5 tsp.)
- Shiitake/crimini mushrooms (1 lb. sliced)
- Red onion (1 chopped)
- Garlic cloves (2)
- Madeira wine (1 cup)
- Sour cream (.5 cup)
- Chicken broth (1 cup)
- Heavy cream (.5 cup)
- Parmesan cheese (.5 cup)

Preparation Directions:

1. Prepare the pasta for about one minute under the package instructions.

2. Melt one tablespoon of butter in the skillet. Add the chicken and cook using the med-high temperature setting for five to seven minutes. Set it aside with the pasta fixings.
3. Add butter (1 tbsp.) to melt and add the mushrooms to sauté for five to seven minutes. Add another tablespoon of butter and add the onions, sautéing for another five minutes or so, using the med-low setting.
4. Mince and mix in the garlic to sauté for one minute. Pour in the wine and chicken broth to simmer for 10-12 minutes until it's reduced (by ¾ of the liquids).
5. Mix in the heavy cream, sour cream, last of the butter (1 tbsp.), and parmesan. Whisk well and add the rest of the fixings.
6. Sprinkle it with more parmesan and serve.

Dinner

Chicken Bellagio

Servings Provided: 5
Total Prep & Cook Time: 50 Minutes

Ingredients:

The Pasta & Sauce:
- Heavy cream (1 cup)
- Cloves of garlic (1 tsp.)
- Parmesan cheese (.5 cup)
- Fresh basil leaves (5-6)
- Juice (1 lemon)
- Black pepper & salt (to taste)
- Thin spaghetti (1 pkg.)

The Chicken:
- Chicken breast (3-4)
- Flour (1 cup)
- Eggs (2)
- Parmesan cheese (1 cup)
- Breadcrumbs - Italian-seasoned (1 cup)
- Oil (vegetable/olive/grapeseed)
  The Garnish:
- Unchilled prosciutto

- Arugula lettuce
- Extra-Virgin olive oil
- Lemons (1-2)

Preparation Directions:

1. Rinse and dry the lettuce. Mince the garlic and basil, and grate the parmesan.
2. Whisk the cream and garlic in a saucepan using a med-high temperature setting until it starts to thicken.
3. Reduce the temperature to med-low. Add in the parmesan, lemon juice, basil, salt, and pepper.
4. To Serve. Toss it with spaghetti that's been prepared using the package instructions (approx. 10 min. al dente).
5. Prep three bowls for the flour whisked eggs, and lastly - the breadcrumbs and parmesan cheese.
6. If the chicken is frozen, thaw it thoroughly. Slice the cutlets in half, so you have two thin pieces.
7. Warm the oil (¾-inch deep) in a skillet using the med-high temperature setting.
8. Dredge the chicken through the flour, egg, and lastly - the breadcrumbs mixture.
9. Place the chicken in the skillet, but don't overcrowd. Cook until browned.
10. Cook until the sides start browning. Turn the chicken over to the second side and cook until done. Place each piece on a layer of paper towels.
11. To serve, place a generous serving of pasta with two pieces of chicken, side-by-side.
12. Slice and add one to two strips of prosciutto and a handful of arugula over the top. Spritz it using oil and juice of a lemon half to serve.

Filet Mignon

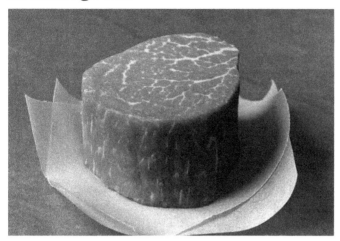

Servings Provided: 2
Total Prep & Cook Time: 2o Minutes

Ingredients:

- Beef tenderloin steaks (2/8 oz. each)
- Butter - divided (3 tbsp.)
- Olive oil (1 tbsp.)
- Merlot (1 cup)
- Salt (1/8 tsp.)
- Heavy whipping cream (2 tbsp.)

Preparation Directions:

1. Warm a small skillet using the medium temperature setting to heat one tablespoon butter and the olive oil. Cook the steak and test the internal temp using a meat thermometer (Medium-well, 145° Fahrenheit; medium-rare at 135° Fahrenheit; and medium, 140° Fahrenheit), four to six minutes per side.
2. Transfer the steaks to a platter and cover them, so they stay warm.
3. Pour the wine into the pan to dislodge the delicious browned bits.

4. Wait for it to boil and adjust the heat to simmer until the liquid is reduced to about ¼ of a cup.
5. Stir in the salt, cream, and remaining butter. Wait for it to boil and simmer, stirring until the butter is melted, and it's slightly thickened (one to two min.). Serve with the steaks.

Dessert

Pumpkin Pecan Cheesecake

Servings Provided: 12
Total Prep & Cook Time: 1 Hr. 45 Min. (+) chill time

Ingredients:

The Crust:
- Ground cinnamon (.25 tsp.)
- Graham cracker crumbs (1.5 cups)
- Unsalted butter (.33 cup)

The Filling:
- Unchilled cream cheese (4 - 8 oz. pkg.)
- Sugar (1.25 cups)
- Sour cream (.5 cup)
- Vanilla extract (2 tsp.)
- Large eggs (5)

The Topping:
- Sugar (2 tsp.)

- Sour cream (.5 cup)
- Also Needed: 9-inch springform pan lined with parchment baking paper

Preparation Directions:

1. Warm the oven to 475° Fahrenheit. Place a large roasting pan of water (½-inch) in the oven.
2. Crush and mix the cracker crumbs and cinnamon, adding the melted butter.
3. Firmly mash the crust in the bottom and about two-thirds up the sides of the prepared pan - lined with paper. Wrap the bottom of the pan using a large piece of aluminum foil. Freeze until the filling is prepared.
4. Use an electric blender to prepare the filling. Measure and add in the sour cream, sugar, cream cheese, and vanilla until it is creamy.
5. Whisk the eggs and mix them in with the cream cheese mixture - until the eggs are incorporated.
6. Scoop in the filling into the prepared crust. Arrange the cheesecake pan in the heated water bath to cook for 12 minutes. Adjust the temperature to 350° Fahrenheit. Bake it until the top of the cheesecake is golden (50 to 60 min.). Transfer it to a wire rack to cool.
7. Mix the sugar and sour cream. Spread it over the cake. Chill it for a minimum of four hours.

Chapter 3

Cracker Barrel™ Favorites

Breakfast

Egg In A Basket

Total Preparation & Cooking Time: 10 Minutes
Servings Provided: 1

Ingredients:

- Sourdough bread (1 slice)
- Margarine/butter (1 tbsp.)
- Egg (1)
- Salt & black pepper (As desired)

Preparation Directions:

1. Heat a skillet using the medium temperature setting. Use a small biscuit cutter to prepare the bread.
2. Spread butter on both sides of the bread and arrange in the pan.
3. To prepare an over-easy egg, toast the bread and drop the cracked egg into the ring as soon as you put the bread into the pan.

4. Otherwise, cook for about a minute before flipping the bread over onto the other side. Cook until the egg is the way you like it.

Fried Apples

Servings Provided: 10
Total Prep & Cook Time: 30 Minutes

Ingredients:

- Butter (3 tbsp.)
- Golden Delicious apples (2 lb./4 medium)
- Granulated sugar (.25 cup)
- Brown sugar (2 tbsp. - tightly packed)
- Nutmeg (.25 tsp.)
- Cinnamon (1 tsp.)
- Apple cider (.5 cup)
- Cornstarch (1 tbsp.)
- Also Needed: 12-inch skillet

Preparation Directions:

1. Melt the butter using the medium temperature function on the stovetop.
2. Core and slice the apples into ¾-inch wedges.
3. Add in the apples, sugars, and spices into the skillet, stirring to coat.
4. Put a top on the skillet and set a timer to cook for 11-14 minutes, until it's tender. Stir the mixture occasionally.
5. Empty the apple mixture into a serving dish and place a plastic film or foil over the top of the dish to keep it warm.
6. Whisk the cornstarch and cider in a small cup and stir it into the same skillet using the medium temperature setting.
7. Simmer the mixture until thickened or for about 30 to 60 seconds. Dump the mixture over the apples before serving.

Hash Brown Casserole

Servings Provided: 12 hashbrowns
Total Prep & Cook Time: 60 Minutes

Ingredients:

- Frozen/thawed hash browns (2 lb.)
- Melted butter (.5 cup)
- Cream of chicken soup (10.75 oz. can)
- Sour cream (1 pint)
- Chopped onion (.5 cup)
- Cheddar cheese (2 cups)
- Pepper (5 tsp.)
- Salt (1 tsp.)
- Also Needed: 11 by 14-inch baking/casserole dish

Preparation Directions:

1. Warm the oven at 350° Fahrenheit. Spray the baking dish with a spritz of cooking oil spray.
2. Grate the cheese and combine all of the fixings in a large mixing container.
3. Spread the mixture into the pan to bake. Set the timer for 45 minutes, cooking until it's nicely browned.

Light & Fluffy Whole Wheat Buttermilk Pancakes With Nuts

Servings Provided: 4 - Varies
Total Prep & Cook Time: 10-15 Minutes

Ingredients:

- Whole wheat & A-P flour (1 cup of each)
- Salt (.5 tsp.)
- A-P flour (1 cup)
- Baking powder (.5 tbsp.)
- Sugar (2 tbsp.)
- Milk (1 cup)
- Buttermilk (.5 cup)
- Melted butter (.25 cup)
- Eggs (2)
- Vanilla (.5 tsp.)
- Suggested Pan: Stainless steel skillet

Preparation Directions:

1. Grease the cold skillet all around with the end of a stick of butter.
2. Set the burner on the stovetop using the medium-low temperature setting.

66

3. Whisk all of the dry components in a mixing container. In another bowl, whisk the wet ones.
4. Whisk the dry and wet fixings until just barely mixed (It will be lumpy.).
5. Scoop out by ¼ cupfuls onto the hot skillet and cook until the entire surface of the pancakes are bubbly, and the edges are dry.
6. Flip and cook for another minute or two. Right before serving, break apart a few pecan halves over the top with your favorite syrup - Cracker Barrel-style.

Lunch

Beef Stew

Servings Provided: 4
Total Prep & Cook Time: 2 Hours

Ingredients:

- Stewing beef - medium-sized chunks (1 lb.
- Vegetable oil - divided (3 tbsp.)
- Salt and pepper (as desired)
- Flour (.5 cup)
- Onion (1 chopped)
- Medium potatoes (4)
- Carrots (5)
- Beef broth (1-quart)
- Ketchup (.33 cup)
- Peas (1 cup)

Preparation Directions:

1. Cut the potatoes and carrots into chunks, after peeling them.
2. Whisk the flour, pepper, and salt. Add the meat, tossing to cover.

3. Measure and add two tablespoons of oil to a large pot to warm using a medium-high temperature setting. Brown the beef in flour (all the flour).
4. Stir often to brown nicely. Transfer the meat onto a platter.
5. Pour in the last bit of oil (1 tbsp.) and sauté the onion until translucent, scraping any browned bits from the pan.
6. Transfer the meat into the pan with the carrots and potatoes. Pour in the stock and ketchup. Stir thoroughly to combine.
7. Simmer over low heat, often stirring for 1.5 hours. Adjust the seasoning to your liking.
8. Add in the frozen peas just before serving. Stir to defrost and serve.

Chicken & Dumplings

Servings Provided: 6
Total Prep & Cook Time: 1.45 Hours – Varies

Ingredients:

- Whole chicken (about 3.5 lb./1 whole)
- Carrots (5)
- Onions (2 medium)
- Bay leaves (2)
- Celery (5 stalks)
- Fresh parsley (4 stalks) or Dry flakes (2 tbsp.)
- Poultry seasoning (1 tsp.)
- Freshly cracked black pepper (.5 tsp.)
- Salt (1 tsp./as needed)
- Flour (2.5 cups)
- Baking powder (3 tsp.)
- Unchilled solid shortening or butter (3 tbsp.)
- Milk (1.25 cups)

Preparation Directions:

1. Prepare a dutch oven with three quarts of water (enough to cover) and add the chicken. Peel the carrots, onion, and celery stalks, all roughly chopped.

2. Fold in half of the parsley, the bay leaves, and the rest of the spices. Once boiling, lower the temperature setting and simmer for 45 minutes. Chop it into bite-size pieces.
3. Toss the chicken in the pot with three cups of stock, plus the celery, salt, pepper, onion, and rest of the carrots (all finely diced). Simmer it for another 15-20 minutes.
4. Sift the flour, salt, and baking powder using your hands or a pastry blender to mix in the butter until crumbly. Add the rest of the chopped parsley milk to form a soft dough.
5. Drop the dough by the spoonful (12)on top of the chicken mixture. Simmer the dumplings with the lid off for about five minutes.
6. Place a lid on the pot and simmer for another 20 minutes before serving.

Dinner

Broccoli Cheddar Chicken

Servings Provided: 4
Total Prep & Cook Time: 55 Minutes

Ingredients:

- Boneless - skinless chicken breast (4)
- Salt & black pepper (.5 tsp. of each)
- Milk (1 cup milk)
- Cheddar cheese soup (1 small can)
- Paprika (.5 tsp.)
- Cheddar cheese (6 oz. - shredded)
- Frozen chopped broccoli (8 oz.)
- Crushed buttery crackers (1.5 cups)

Preparation Directions:

1. Warm the oven at 350° Fahrenheit and lightly grease a baking dish.
2. Sprinkle the chicken using pepper and salt, adding it to the dish.

3. Mix the soup, milk, cheddar cheese, and paprika. Dump about half of the mixture and broccoli pieces over the chicken.
4. Top with the crunched crackers and the rest of the cheese mixture.
5. Set a timer and bake it for 45 minutes. Serve with your favorite side dish.

Grilled Chicken Tenderloins

Servings Provided: 4
Total Prep & Cook Time: 1 ¼ Hours

Ingredients:

- Chicken tenderloin (1 lb.)
- Italian dressing (.5 cup)
- Honey (1.5 tsp.)
- Fresh lime juice (1 tsp.)

Preparation Directions:

1. Whisk the honey and juice to make the dressing. Toss it into a zipper-type baggie and marinate the chicken in the fridge for 60 minutes.
2. Warm a skillet (med.temp) with a spritz of cooking oil spray.
3. Add the chicken and cook about eight minutes total (internal temp of 165° Fahrenheit).
4. Serve with your preferred veggies.

Homestyle Chicken

Total Prep & Cook Time: 15-20 Minutes
Servings Provided: 4

Ingredients:

- To Fry: Oil (as needed)
- Chicken breast: skinless & boneless (4)
- All-purpose flour (2 cups)
- Salt & freshly cracked black pepper (2 tsp. of each)
- Water (.5 cup)
- Buttermilk (1 cup)

Preparation Directions:

1. Prepare a large pot/deep fryer with about three to four inches of oil. Set the temperature of a deep fryer at 350° Fahrenheit.
2. Make the chicken about the same size by placing them between two layers of wax paper. Pound them with a meat mallet to help with uniform cooking. Pat them dry with a paper towel.
3. Prepare the seasoned flour using salt, pepper, and flour. Whisk or sift it thoroughly.
4. Mix the water and buttermilk in another mixing container.

5. Prepare the chicken with pepper and salt, dredge them in the flour, buttermilk, and the flour until covered.
6. Cook them for seven to eight minutes and drain on a wire rack. Serve with your favorite side dish.

Meatloaf

Servings Provided: 4
Total Prep & Cook Time: 1 Hr. 20 Min.

Ingredients:

- Onion (1)
- Green pepper (1)
- Ground beef (1 lb.)
- Diced tomatoes (1 can)
- Egg (1)
- Frozen biscuits - grated (.5 cup)
- Salt (1 tsp.)
- Ketchup (.25 cup)

Preparation Instructions:

1. Set the oven temperature at 350° Fahrenheit.
2. Use a box grater to prepare the frozen biscuits. Dice the onions and peppers.
3. Combine all of the fixings (omit the ketchup).
4. Lightly spritz a loaf pan using a cooking oil spray. Add the beef mixture. Bake the meatloaf for one hour and 15 minutes.
5. Transfer the baking tray from the oven and wait for about ten minutes.

6. Drain the juices from the pan and place the meatloaf onto a serving platter.
7. Garnish the meatloaf with ketchup and serve.

Side Dish

Loaded Potato Salad

Total Prep & Cook Time: 35 Minutes
Servings Provided: 3-4

Ingredients:

- Cooked potatoes (3 large)
- Hard-boiled eggs (3)
- Minced onion (4 tbsp.)
- Black pepper (as desired)
- Dry mustard (1 tsp.)
- Salt (1 tsp.)
  The Saucepan:
- Eggs (2 uncooked)
- Sugar (3 tsp.)
- Melted butter (3 tbsp.)
- Hot vinegar (.5 cup)
- Mayonnaise (1 cup)

Preparation Directions:

1. Mix the potatoes, eggs, onion, mustard, salt, and pepper.

2. Measure and add the sugar, vinegar, eggs, and melted butter in a saucepan and simmer until thickened.
3. Combine with the mayonnaise and served.

Dessert

Ambrosia Fruit Salad

Total Prep & Cook Time: 15 Minutes
Servings Provided: 4-6

Ingredients:

- Oranges (6)
- Pineapple chunks (1 can)
- Coconut (.25 lb.)
- Apples (2)
- For the Garnish: Sugar

Preparation Directions:

1. Peel and cut the oranges into chunks and chop the apples.
2. Make the salad by alternating the layers in serving bowls as desired - chilled.

Banana Pudding

Servings Provided:
Total Prep & Cook Time: 1.5 Hours

Ingredients:

- Quart milk (1.5 quarts)
- Eggs (5)
- Vanilla extract (.25 tsp.)
- Flour (1 ⅛ cups)
- Sugar (1.5 cups)
- Vanilla wafers (12 oz.)
- Bananas (3 peeled)
- Cool Whip (8 oz.)

Preparation Directions:

1. Heat milk to 170° Fahrenheit.
2. Briskly beat the eggs with the vanilla, sugar, and flour in a mixing container. Slowly combine it with the milk and cook until thick and custard-like.
3. Layer the wafers on the bottom of a baking pan.
4. Slice the bananas and layer over the wafers.
5. Pour the custard over the wafers and bananas. Cool the pudding for 1.5 hours.
6. Spread the topping over the pudding to serve.

Chocolate Cherry Cobbler

Servings Provided: 6
Total Prep & Cook Time: 55-60 Minutes

Ingredients:

- Cherry pie filling (21 oz. can)
- A-P flour (1.5 cups)
- Sugar (.5 cup)Salt (.5 tsp.)
- Baking powder (2 tsp.)
- Cold butter (.25 cup or half of 1 stick)
- Egg (1)
- Evaporated milk (.25 cup)
- Chocolate chips (6 oz. bag or 1 cup)
- Slivered almonds (.5 cup)
- Suggested: 1.5 to a 2-quart oval baking dish

Preparation Directions:

1. Warm the oven at 350° Fahrenheit.
2. Sift the baking powder, sugar, salt, and flour into a mixing container. Dice the butter, mixing it in until it's pea-sized. Set it aside for now.
3. Dump the filling into the baking dish. Set it aside also.

83

4. Melt and stir the chocolate chips using the microwave or stovetop. Cool it down for about five minutes. Pour and stir in the milk and egg.
5. Combine the flour and chocolate fixings, and drop them into the cherry filling in the baking dish.
6. Sprinkle using the almonds and set the timer for 40 to 45 minutes.
7. When the timer buzzes, transfer the pan from the oven and serve warm with a portion of ice cream or whipped cream.

Chapter 4

Olive Garden™ Favorites

Brunch Favorites

Cheesy Stuffed Sausage Bread

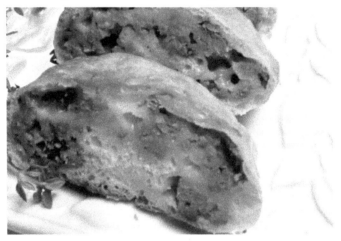

Servings Provided: 12
Total Prep & Cook Time: 40 Minutes

Ingredients:

- Johnsonville Mild Italian Sausage (2 pkg./1 kg.)
- Red pepper flakes (as desired)
- Italian seasoning (1 tsp.)
- Salt and pepper to taste
- Green pepper (1 diced)
- Large white onion (half of 1 - diced)
- White mushrooms, sliced (12 medium to large)
- Pizza sauce (398 ml./13.5 oz.)
- Large French loaf of bread
- Mozzarella cheese (3-4 cups)

Preparation Directions:

1. Fry the sausage with the pepper flakes, salt, black pepper until browned.

2. Remove the sausage from the pan, leaving in about one tablespoon of the drippings or one tablespoon of olive oil.
3. Sauté the green pepper, onion, and mushrooms until softened.
4. Add the sausage back in and the pizza sauce. Simmer it for about ten minutes with a lid on it. If it is too thin, let it reduce with the lid off.
5. Meanwhile, slice the loaf in half and pull out some of the middle of the bread.
6. Place the hot sausage mixture in the two halves of the bread.
7. Top with lots of cheese and broil it until melted. Slice and serve hot.

Chicken & Shrimp Carbonara

Total Prep & Cook Time: 60 Minutes
Servings Provided: 6

Ingredients:

- Chicken breast halves (1 lb.)
- Olive oil - divided (4 tbsp.)
- Minced garlic - divided (3 tbsp.)
- Italian seasoning (2 tbsp.)
- Jumbo shrimp (1 lb.)
- Linguine pasta (16 oz. pkg.)
- Smoked bacon - diced (8 slices)
- Onion (1 diced)
- Heavy whipping cream (1.5 cups)
- Egg yolks (4)
- Parmesan cheese (1.5 cups - grated)
- Salt & ground black pepper (1 pinch/to taste)
- Sauvignon Blanc wine (.25 cup)

Preparation Directions:

1. Peel and devein the shrimp and dice the bacon. Discard the bones and skin from the chicken. Chop it into bite-sized pieces.

2. Prepare a skillet to warm one tablespoon of oil using the med-high temperature setting. Cook and stir chicken with one tablespoon of garlic and one tablespoon of Italian seasoning (6-8 min.). Dump the chicken into a bowl for now.
3. Warm one tablespoon garlic and one tablespoon olive oil in the same pan. Fry the shrimp until it's a pinkish-red on the outside and white on the inside (6-8 min.). Place it with the chicken.
4. Add water to a large pot and wait for it to boil. Add the rest of the oil (two tablespoons). Cook the linguine until it's al dente (10-12 min.). Dump it into a colander to drain.
5. Toss the bacon into the pan to cook until it's just crispy, not crunchy (6 min.). Drain on two paper towels. Sauté the onion in the bacon grease until translucent (about 5 min.).
6. While the onion is sauteing, mix the cream, parmesan cheese, egg yolks, salt, pepper, and rest of the Italian seasoning in a mixing bowl.
7. Pour wine into the pan with the onions. Increase the temperature setting and wait for it to boil. Simmer it until the wine is mostly evaporated (about 2 min.). Add the creamy egg mixture and reduce heat. Simmer until sauce begins to thicken (3-5 min.). Add the chicken and shrimp; mix to coat. Serve on top of a platter of pasta.

Delicious Fresh Breadsticks

Servings Provided: 8-10
Total Prep & Cook Time: 2.5 Hours – Varies

Ingredients:

- Frozen - thawed bread dough (1 loaf @ room temp)
- Garlic powder (as desired)
- Vegetable cooking oil spray
- Oregano (leaves - rubbed to a fine powder with fingers)

Preparation Directions:

1. Lightly spritz a baking sheet using the cooking oil.
2. When thawed, spray your hands with the oil spray and knead the dough into 8-10 cigar-sized sticks.
3. Arrange them about three inches apart on the baking tray. Place them in a warm area to rise until they are about doubled in size (1.5-2 hrs.)
4. Lightly spray and dust each one with oregano and garlic powder.
5. Bake them for 20 to 25 minutes. Transfer them to a wire rack to thoroughly cool.
6. Enjoy them for one or two days.

Grilled Chicken Flatbread

Total Prep & Cook Time: 45 Minutes
Servings Provided: 4

Ingredients:

- Cooking oil (1 tbsp.)
- Flatbread (12 oz.)
- Chicken breast (.5 lb.)
- Alfredo sauce/your choice (1 cup)
- Grilled red pepper (1)
- Freshly chopped basil (.25 cup)
- Mozzarella cheese (.25 cup shredded)
- Garlic clove (1)

Preparation Directions:

1. Sprinkle the chicken with pepper and salt.
2. Prepare a skillet to warm the oil using the med-low temperature setting.
3. Cook the chicken for six minutes, flip it over and continue cooking for another five to six minutes. Cool it slightly and slice it into small slices.
4. Warm the oven at 350° Fahrenheit.
5. Peel the garlic clove, slice it in half and rub it over the bread.

6. Place the sliced chicken on the bred and cover it using the Alfredo sauce. Top it off with about half of the grilled peppers and a sprinkle of mozzarella over the tops.
7. Bake it in the hot oven for about six to eight minutes.
8. Remove and top it with the rest of the peppers and basil to serve.

Grilled Chicken With Peach Sauce

Servings Provided: 8
Total Prep & Cook Time: 40 Minutes

Ingredients:

- Chicken breast (8 halves)
- Black pepper & salt (1 pinch of each - to taste)
- Garlic (1 tbsp.)
- Olive oil (3 tbsp.)
- Peach preserves (2 cups)
- Dijon-style mustard (1 tbsp.)
- Soy sauce (2 tbsp.)
- Ripe peaches (4)

Preparation Directions:

1. Warm the grill using the medium temperature setting and lightly oil the grate. Discard the bones and skin from the chicken and sprinkle with the black pepper and salt.
2. Carefully arrange the chicken on the hot grill, and cook until browned as desired (6-7 min.) and flip it. Continue cooking for five to six minutes.
3. Finely dice the garlic. Prepare the sauce and brush both sides of the chicken. Simmer it for four to five

93

minutes. Use an instant-read thermometer to test in the center-most part of the breast. It should read at least 165° Fahrenheit.

4. Slice and arrange the peach halves cut-side down on the grill to cook for about two minutes. Turn them over and brush with the rest of the peach sauce. Grill them for another three to four minutes.

Lunch

Broccoli & Pasta

Servings Provided: 4
Total Prep & Cook Time: 25-30 Minutes

Ingredients:

- Cooked pasta shells (1 lb.
- Olive oil (.25 cup)
- Broccoli florets (12 oz.)
- Minced garlic (2 tsp.)
- Green onions (.25 cup)
- Mushrooms (1 cup)
- Fresh parsley (2 tsp.)
- Grated parmesan cheese (as desired)

  The Sauce:
- Flour (.25 cup)
- Margarine/butter (.25 cup)
- Milk (1 quart)
- Mashed chicken bouillon cubes (2 tsp.)

Preparation Directions:

1. Prepare the sauce. Melt the butter in a two-quart saucepan using the medium temperature setting.
2. Steam the broccoli and cook the pasta. Mince the garlic and slice the mushrooms and onions.
3. Stir in the flour to simmer for one minute. Pour in the milk and bouillon, whisking vigorously with a whisk. Once boiling, adjust the heat to a simmer for five minutes (often stirring). Leave it on warm.
4. Drain the broccoli, divide in half, removing half of the florets into ¼-inch pieces.
5. Warm the oil using the medium temperature setting. Toss in the mushrooms, onions, garlic, and broccoli into the pan of hot oil. Sauté for two minutes and add the parsley.
6. Combine everything and garnish with a dusting of parmesan.

Gnocchi Soup

Servings Provided: 8
Total Prep & Cook Time: 35-40 Minutes

Ingredients:

- Olive oil (1 tbsp.)
- Butter (4 tbsp.)
- Onion (1 cup)
- Cloves of garlic (2)
- Celery (.5 cup)
- All-purpose flour (.25 cup)
- Half & Half (1 quart)
- Chicken broth (28 oz.)
- Dried parsley & thyme (.5 tsp. of each)
- Optional: Ground nutmeg (.25 tsp.)
- Carrots (1 cup)
- Spinach leaves (1 cup)
- Chicken breast (1 cup - cooked)
- Gnocchi (16 oz. ready to use pkg.)

Preparation Directions:

1. Finely dice the cooked chicken, onion, garlic, and celery. Finely shred the carrots and coarsely chop the spinach.

2. Warm a large saucepan to melt the butter and oil. Toss in the celery, garlic, and onion to sauté for a few minutes until translucent.
3. Whisk and mix in the flour to sauté for one minute. Measure and mix in the Half & Half. Simmer further until it's thickened.
4. Mix in the broth and simmer, stirring in salt, parsley thyme, nutmeg, gnocchi, chicken, spinach, and carrots
   Simmer until it's hot and serve it right away.

Olive Garden's Healthy Spaghetti Sauce

Servings Provided: 6-8
Total Prep & Cook Time: 25 Minutes

Ingredients:

- Ground round (2 lb.)
- Oil (2 tbsp.)
- Stewed/cut-up tomatoes (14 oz. can)
- V-8 Juice (6 oz.)
- Prego spaghetti sauce (16 oz. jar)
- Onion soup mix (1 envelope)
- Grape jelly (.5 cup)

Preparation Directions:

1. Brown the meat in a skillet, crumbling as it cooks until browned.
2. Dump in the jelly, soup mix, Prego, V-8, and tomatoes.
3. Stir and simmer for 15-20 minutes until it's steamy hot.
4. Serve it with your favorite pasta.

Zuppa Toscana Soup

Servings Provided: 10
Total Prep & Cook Time: 35 Minutes

Ingredients:

- Ground hot sausage (1 lb.)
- Garlic cloves (3)
- Medium onion (1)
- Flour (1 tbsp.)
- Chicken broth (2 - 32 oz. cartons)
- Russet potatoes (6)
- Heavy cream (1 cup)
- Kale pieces (6 cups - torn)

Preparation Directions:

1. Crumble and toss the sausage into a large soup pot using the medium temperature setting. Once browning, mince, and add in the diced onion and garlic. After the onions are translucent, sprinkle them using the flour and mix in the broth. Wait for it to boil.
2. Wash the potatoes thoroughly and cut them into halves lengthwise (¼-inch slices). Toss them into the boiling pot and simmer until done (20 min.).

3. Set the heat to low. Mix in the heavy cream and toss the kale into the pot. Simmer for about five minutes, occasionally stirring before serving.

Dinner

Chicken Piccata

Servings Provided: 5
Total Prep & Cook Time: 30-35 Minutes

Ingredients:

- Pounded chicken breasts (4/0.25-inch thickness/2 lb.)
- Onion (1 small)
- Sun-dried tomatoes in strips (10)
- Garlic (1 minced)
- Chicken broth (1 tbsp.)
- Juiced lemon (2 tbsp./half of 1)
- Rinsed capers (.25 cup)
- Butter (3 tbsp.)
- Heavy cream (.33 cup)
- For Frying: Olive oil (4 tbsp.)
- Black pepper and salt (as desired)

Preparation Directions:

1. Pound the chicken with a mallet and dust it using pepper and salt.

102

2. Pour the oil into a pan and fry the chicken using the med-high temperature setting (5-8 min. per side). Take them from the skillet and put them in a covered container for now.
3. Toss in the onion, tomatoes, and garlic into the same pan to sauté until they are a golden brown (1-2 min.). Whisk in the lemon juice, chicken broth, and capers. Scoot the browned bits in the pan and continue cooking them for 10-15 minutes (med-low) until it's reduced by about half in volume.
4. Once the sauce is thickened, take the pan off of the burner and mix in the butter until it's melted. Then, mix in the cream.
5. Heat the mixture thoroughly and combine with the chicken to reheat. Cover the chicken in sauce and serve.
6. Note: You can also use one to two tablespoons of the sun-dried tomato oil for part of the olive oil for a flavor change.

Steak Gorgonzola

Servings Provided: 4
Total Prep & Cook Time: 45 Minutes

Ingredients:

The Steak:
- Steak medallions - ex.eye of round (1 lb.)
- Balsamic vinegar (1 tbsp.)
- Black pepper and salt (as desired)

The Alfredo:
- Fettuccine (1 lb.)
- Unsalted butter (1 stick/.25 lb.)
- Heavy cream (2 cups)
- Spinach (2 cups)
- Nutmeg (.25 tsp.)
- Parmesan cheese (1 cup)
- Salt and pepper (as desired)
- Gorgonzola crumbles (4 oz.)

The Toppings:
- Balsamic glaze (4 tbsp.)
- Sun-dried tomatoes (.25 cup)
- Gorgonzola crumbles (2 oz.)

Preparation Directions:

1. Dust the steak with salt and pepper. Toss it into a zipper-type bag with the balsamic vinegar. Close the bag and marinate it for 30 minutes to four hours.
2. Warm a cast-iron skillet using the medium temperature heat setting. Add the prepared steak and cook until it's done as desired. Cover in a plate using a tent of foil. (It will continue cooking, so stop cooking a couple of minutes before it's as you like it.)
3. Cook the rest of the fixings.
4. Start the pasta water and prepare it until it is almost al dente. Drain and set it aside, reserving one cup of the liquids to thin the sauce as needed.
5. Melt the butter and cream in a skillet using the medium temperature setting. After it's melted, reduce the setting to med-low.
6. Fold in the nutmeg and spinach to wilt (5 min.).
7. Sprinkle it with the parmesan, pepper, and salt. Mix in the pasta with the sauce.
8. Toss it and cook for two to three minutes.
9. Transfer the pasta from the hot burner and add the gorgonzola cheese. Toss and serve.
10. Top each of the medallions of steak with the balsamic glaze, tomatoes, and gorgonzola crumbles.

Tuscan Chicken - Keto-Friendly

Servings Provided: 4
Total Prep & Cook Time: 50 Minutes

Ingredients:

- Chicken thighs (1-2 lb.)
- Olive oil (1 tbsp. + 2 tbsp for the dutch oven)
- Garlic (3 tbsp.)
- Chicken broth (.33 cup)
- Heavy cream (1 cup)
- Freshly grated parmesan cheese (.75 cup)
- Italian seasoning (1 tbsp.)
- Red pepper flakes (2 tsp.)
- Kosher salt & black pepper (.5 tsp.each)
- Sun-dried tomatoes (.33 cup)
- Fresh spinach (2 cups)

Preparation Directions:

1. Warm one tablespoon of the oil in a saucepan using the med-high temperature setting. Mince and add the garlic to sauté until it's lightly browned (2 min.).
2. Stir in the chicken broth and heavy cream, bringing it to a slow boil.

3. Lower the temperature as needed, and continue cooking it for about ten minutes until the sauce starts thickening.
4. Pour in about two tablespoons of oil into the dutch oven and add the thighs.
5. Sprinkle the pepper flakes, Italian seasoning, kosher salt, ground pepper, and tomatoes. Sprinkle in the parmesan and whisk until it's smooth.
6. Pour the sauce over the chicken and lower the temperature setting to low.
7. Cook it for another half an hour to one hour if possible.
8. Remove the chicken and add the spinach. Cook until it's wilted. Fold the chicken back into the pan and cook for ten more minutes. Add the sauce over the dish to serve.
9. If you are watching your calories and nutrients, each portion is 612 calories, nine net carbs, 28g of protein, and 51g of fat.

Delicious Beverage

Limoncello Lemonade

Servings Provided: 1
Total Prep & Cook Time: 5 Minutes

Ingredients:

- Hot water (.25 cup)
- Granulated sugar (.25 cup)
- Smirnoff Citrus Vodka (1 oz.)
- Lemon juice (4 tsp.)
- Limoncelli liqueur (1 oz.)
- Lemonade - ex. Country Time/Minute Maid (4 oz.)
- Ice (1-2 cups)
- To Garnish: Lemon slice

Preparation Directions:

1. Prepare the lemon syrup (juice, sugar, and hot water).
2. Once the mixture is cooled, prepare the drink by combining .75 ounce of the syrup with the lemonade, limoncello, and vodka.
3. Blend using the high-speed setting until it's slushy.
4. Serve with a lemon slice on the rim and a straw.

Dessert

Chef John's Zabaglione

Servings Provided: 2
Total Prep & Cook Time: 1.25-1.5 Hours

Ingredients:

- Strawberries (.5 cup)
- White sugar (1 tsp. + 3 tbsp.)
- Egg yolks (3 large)
- Dry Marsala wine (.25 cup)

Preparation Directions:

1. Remove the hulls, slice the strawberries into halves, and mix them with the sugar (1 tsp.). Cover the bowl and let it rest on the countertop for about one hour.
2. Portion fruit into two serving bowls of choice.
3. Toss the yolks of the eggs, sugar, and marsala into a metal mixing container. Heat it using the low-temperature setting. As it heats, whisk until it forms loose peaks (6-8 min.) and warm to the touch.
4. Scoop the custard over the berries and serve warm.

Raspberry Mousse Cheesecake

Servings Provided: 6
Total Prep & Cook Time: The Crust: 30 Minutes/The Pie:
45 Minutes

Ingredients:

The Crust:
- Chocolate cookie crumbs - ex. Nabisco
  Wafers/Chocolate part Oreos - ground (1.5 cups)
- Granulated sugar (2 tbsp.)
- Melted unsalted butter (1/3 cup)

The Filling:
- Unchilled cream cheese (1 lb.)
- Sugar (.5 cup)
- Eggs (2)
- Vanilla extract (.5 tsp.)

The Mousse:
- Gelatin (1.5 tsp.)
- Water - cold (1.5 tbsp.)
- Heavy whipping cream (1 cup)
- Raspberry preserves (.5 cup)
- Sugar (2 tbsp.)
- Also Needed Nine-inch pie pan

Preparation Directions:

1. Prepare the crust. Warm the oven to 350° Fahrenheit.
2. Combine the crunched cookies, sugar, and melted butter. Stir until thoroughly mixed. Pour the chocolate crumbs into the pan. Press it firmly across the bottom and against the sides of the pie pan.
3. Set a timer to bake it for ten minutes. Do not overcook it. Transfer it to a wire rack to thoroughly cool.
4. Make the filling. Adjust the oven temperature to 325° Fahrenheit.
5. Mix the eggs, sugar, cream cheese, and vanilla using an electric mixer (3-4 min.)
6. Dump it into the crust to bake for 25 minutes. Cool in the fridge.
7. Prepare the mousse by sprinkling the gelatin over cold water to stand for one minute. Microwave for 30 seconds on the high setting until it's dissolved or add one tablespoon of water to heat on the stovetop.
8. Mix the preserves with the gelatin and chill for about ten minutes.
9. Whip the cream to form soft peaks and add two tablespoons of sugar. Whip until you have 1.5 cups of cream for the mouse.
10. Refrigerate the rest of the cream for topping.
11. Fold the raspberry into the measured whipped cream and spread it over the chilled cheesecake. Scoop it in the center of the cake to spread. Shill for one hour before serving.
12. Slice it into six servings with a dollop of the reserved whipped cream.

Tiramisu

Servings Provided: 10
Total Prep & Cook Time: 40 Minutes

Ingredients:

- Sponge cake (about 12 slices - 3-inches high)
- Black coffee - strong-brew (3 oz.)
- Rum/brandy (3 oz.)
- Unchilled cream cheese (1.5 lb.)
- Super-fine sugar (1.5 cups)
- The Topping: Cocoa powder

Preparation Directions:

1. Slice the cake into two layers (1.5-inch thick each).
2. Whisk the brandy and coffee and drizzle it over the bottom half of the cake (just to flavor it).
3. Whisk the cheese and one cup of sugar until combined and spreadable.
4. Spread half of the cheese mixture on the cut side of the cake and add the layer, topping with the rest of the cheese fixings.
5. Sift a bit of cocoa over the top and chill it for about two hours (minimum) before slicing to serve.

Chapter 5

P.F. Chang's™ Favorites

Brunch

Chicken Lettuce Wraps

Total Prep & Cook Time: 20 Minutes
Servings Provided: 4

Ingredients:

- Vegetable oil - divided (4 tbsp.)
- Ground chicken breast (1 lb.)
- Baby Bella mushrooms (o.75 cup)
- Diced water chestnuts (8 oz. can.)
- Diced green onions (4)
- Diced garlic cloves (3)
- Rice vinegar (1 tsp.)
- Hoisin sauce (1 tbsp.)
- Chili paste (2 tsp.)
- Sugar (1 tsp.)
- Soy sauce (Approx. 2 tbsp. + more for serving)
- Cornstarch (2 tsp.)
- Rice noodles (1 oz.)
- For Frying: Oil
- Lettuce leaves (for the wraps)

Preparation Directions:

114

1. Warm a wok using the high-temperature setting and add in the oil (2 tbsp.) and chicken. Stir fry until it's done. Transfer it to a platter and set it aside for now.
2. Pour in the rest of the oil into the wok and continue using the high-temperature setting. Next, dice and toss in the water chestnuts, mushrooms, garlic, onions, and chili paste, continuously stirring (2 min.). Return the chicken to the wok.
3. Stir the hoisin, cornstarch, soy sauce, sugar, and vinegar in a mixing container and put it to the wok. Simmer the mixture an additional minute. Transfer it from the heat and keep warm in the wok.
4. Heat one inch of oil in a skillet to 375° Fahrenheit.
5. Chop the rice noodles and toss them into the skillet. Fry them until crispy (1 min.). Remove the excess oil on a paper-lined platter.
6. Serve the stir-fry and noodles wrapped in the leaves of lettuce.

Orange Beef Lettuce Wraps

Servings Provided: 8
Total Prep & Cook Time: 35 Minutes

Ingredients:

The Sauce:
- Rice vinegar (.25 cup)
- Soy sauce - Reduced-sodium (1 tbsp.)
- Water (3 tbsp.)
- Orange marmalade (3 tbsp.)
- Sugar (1 tbsp.)
- Minced garlic cloves (2)
- Sriracha chili sauce (1 tsp.)

The Wraps:
- Ground beef - 90% lean (1.5 lb.)
- Garlic (2 cloves)
- Ginger root (2 tsp.)
- Soy sauce - Reduced-sodium (.25 cup)
- Sugar (1 tbsp.)
- Orange juice (2 tbsp.)
- Cornstarch (2 tsp.)

- Red pepper flakes - crushed (.25 tsp.)
- Orange marmalade (1 tbsp.)
- Water (.25 cup - cold)
- Boston/Bibb lettuce (8 leaves)
- Cooked brown rice (2 cups)
- Thinly sliced green onions (3)
- Shredded carrots (1 cup)

Preparation Directions:

1. Mince the garlic and ginger. Measure and whisk the sauce fixings in a mixing container.
2. Sauté the garlic, ginger, and beef in a large skillet using the medium temperature setting for eight to ten minutes. (The pink should be gone). Break the beef into crumbles and drain.
3. Stir in orange juice, soy sauce, marmalade, sugar, and pepper flakes.
4. Whisk the water and cornstarch in a small mixing container and stir it into the skillet. Simmer and stir the mixture until the sauce is thickened or for one to two minutes.
5. Prepare the lettuce leaves with rice. Top them off using carrots and green onions, and a drizzle of the sauce.

Pad Thai - Vegetarian

Servings Provided: 4
Total Prep & Cook Time: 30-35 Minutes

Ingredients:

- Thick rice noodles (6 oz. - uncooked)
- Soy sauce - reduced-sodium (3 tbsp.)
- Olive oil (2 tsp.)
- Lime juice (2 tsp.)
- Rice vinegar (4 tsp.)
- Packed brown sugar (2 tbsp.)
- Shredded carrots (3 medium)
- Sweet red peppers - in strips (1 medium)
- Garlic cloves (3)
- Green onions (4)
- Lightly whisked eggs (4 large)
- Bean sprouts (2 cups)
- Freshly chopped cilantro (.33 cups)
- Optional: Chopped peanuts
- Lime wedges
- Also Needed: 12-inch non-stick skillet

Preparation Directions:

1. Prepare the noodles. Drain them in a colander and rinse thoroughly, draining again.
2. Whisk the vinegar, brown sugar, soy sauce, and lime juice.
3. Prepare the skillet to warm the oil using the med-high temperature setting. Stir-fry the carrots and pepper until crispy (3 to 4 min.). Chop/mince the garlic and green onions, and continue sautéing for about two minutes. Transfer the mix from the pan.
4. Lower the temperature setting to medium.
5. Dump the eggs into the same pan and cook until no liquid egg remains. Stir in the noodles, carrot mixture, and sauce mixture. Warm the mixture thoroughly. Fold in the bean sprouts, tossing to mix.
6. Top it off with cilantro, peanuts, and lime wedges.

Lunch

China Bistro Specialty

Servings Provided: 1
Total Prep & Cook Time: 3 Hours

Ingredients:

- Beef sirloin (1.5 lb.)
- Garlic powder (as desired)
- Vegetable oil (2.5 tbsp.)
- Beef bouillon (1 tsp/1 cube)
- Hot water (.25 cup)
- Cornstarch (.5 tbsp.)
- Onion (.33 cup)
- Bell peppers (1 green & 1 red)
- Stewed tomatoes (half of a 7 oz. can - with the juices)
- Soy sauce (2.5 tbsp.)
- White sugar (1 tsp.)
- Salt (.5 tsp.)

Preparation Directions:

1. Slice the beef into 1-inch wide by 1.5-inch long strips (across the grain).
2. Chop the red and green peppers with the onions into cubes. Mix in the garlic powder.
3. Dissolve the bouillon in hot water, mixing in the cornstarch.
4. Warm a skillet or wok using the medium temperature setting. Add the oil and stir-fry the seasoned beef cubes.
5. Dump the mixture into a crockpot. Stir in the bouillon mixture. Add the rest of the fixings and cover with a lid. Set a timer for six to eight hours on low or three to four hours using the high setting.
6. Serve the steak with noodles or rice.

Garlic Noodles

Servings Provided: 2
Total Prep & Cook Time: Under 30 Minutes

Ingredients:

- Chinese noodles/vermicelli (1 lb. fresh)
- Red chile flakes (1.5 tsp.)
- Chopped cilantro (2 tsp.)
- Japanese cucumber or English cucumber (1)
- Canola oil (2 tsp.)
- Garlic (3 tsp. - minced)
- Sugar (3 tsp.)
- White vinegar (2 tsp.)
- Cantonese stir fry sauce - below (4 oz.)
- Sesame oil (.5 tsp.)

    The Sauce:
- Water (.75 cup)
- Sugar (1 tsp.)
- Chicken base powder (1 tsp.)
- Shaohsing wine/Sherry (2 tsp.)
- Oyster sauce (1 tsp.)
- Salt (.5 tsp.)
- Cornstarch (1 tsp.)

Preparation Directions:

1. Cook and rinse the pasta. Mix in the cilantro and chile flakes.
2. Rinse the cucumber and diagonally slice it into ¼-inch pieces.
3. Warm the wok to heat the oil and briefly stir-fry the minced garlic. Add in the sugar and vinegar.
4. Add the noodle and stir fry sauce to the wok, stirring to mix until the noodles are heated thoroughly.
5. Serve them on plates and with cucumber strips and a sprinkle of sesame oil.
6. The Stir Fry Sauce: Combine all of the sauce fixings until smooth and well blended.

Dinner

Asian Slow-Cooked Short Ribs

Servings Provided: 4
Total Prep & Cook Time: 6 Hours 10 Minutes

Ingredients:

- Bone-in beef short ribs (8/4 lb.)
- Stewed tomatoes (28 oz. can)
- Medium onion (1)
- Garlic cloves (4)
- Soy sauce (2 tbsp.)
- Bay leaves (2)
- Worcestershire sauce (1 tbsp.)
- Honey (2 tbsp.)
- Chili garlic sauce (1 tbsp.)
- Pepper (1 tsp.)
- Salt (.5 tsp.)
- Optional: Hot rice

Preparation Directions:

1. Chop the onion and mince the garlic cloves.

2. In a four or five-quart slow cooker, combine the first ten fixings.
3. Add the short ribs, and set the cooker using the low setting to cook until meat is tender (6-8) hours).
4. Discard the bay leaves and serve with a portion of rice.

Beef & Broccoli

Servings Provided: 2
Total Prep & Cook Time: ½ hour

Ingredients:

- Cornstarch (1 tbsp.)
- Low-sodium beef broth (.5 cup)
- Sherry/more beef broth (.25 cup)
- Soy sauce (2 tbsp.)
- Brown sugar (1 tbsp.)
- Garlic (1 clove)
- Ginger root (1 tsp.)
- Canola oil - divided (2 tsp.)
- Beef top sirloin steak - ¼-inch strips (.5 lb.)
- Broccoli - small florets (2 cups)
- Green onions - 1-inch pieces (8)

Preparation Directions:

1. Mince the ginger and garlic. Mix the first seven ingredients. Prepare a large nonstick skillet using the med-high temperature setting.
2. Pour in one teaspoon of oil into the pan to heat. Stir-fry the beef until browned (one to three min.). Remove them from the pan.

3. Stir-fry the broccoli in the rest of the oil until it is crispy and tender (three to five min.). Add the green onions and simmer until it is slightly tender (one to two min).
4. Whisk the cornstarch mixture and add it to the skillet. Wait for the mixture to boil. Continue cooking until the sauce is thickened (two to three min.). Fold in the beef and heat thoroughly.

California Roll

Servings Provided: 64 pieces
Total Prep & Cook Time: 60 Minutes (+) Waiting time

Ingredients:

- Rinsed sushi rice (2 cups)
- Water (2 cups)
- Rice vinegar (.25 cup)
- Sugar (2 tbsp.)
- Toasted sesame seeds (2 tbsp.)
- Salt (.5 tsp.)
- Black sesame seeds (2 tbsp.)
- Nori sheets** (8)
- Peeled & julienned ripe avocado (1 medium)
- Bamboo sushi mat
- Optional: Reduced-sodium - soy sauce - pickled ginger slices, and prepared wasabi

Preparation Directions:

1. Rinse and drain the sushi rice. Prepare a large saucepan and mix the rice and water to stand for about half an hour. Wait for it to boil—lower the temperature setting to low. Put a top on the pan

and continue cooking it slowly until the rice water is incorporated (for 15-20 min.).

2. Transfer the saucepan to a cool burner. Allow the mixture rest, with a lid *on* for ten minutes.

3. Meanwhile, whisk the salt, sugar, and vinegar in a small mixing container. Continue to stir until the sugar is dissolved.

4. Dump the rice into a large shallow bowl and spritz it using the vinegar mixture.

5. Stir the rice using a wooden spoon with a chopping motion until it is slightly cooled. Cover it using a damp tea towel to hold the moisture.

6. Sprinkle both types of sesame seeds onto a platter, and set them aside for now.

7. Place a sushi mat on a work surface, lining it using a layer of plastic wrap.

8. Place ¾ cup of rice onto the plastic. Press the rice into an eight-inch square. Add one of the nori sheets.

9. Arrange a minimal portion of avocado, crab, and cucumber about 1.5 inches from the nori sheet's bottom edge.

10. Roll the rice mixture over the filling and dredge the rolls through the prepared platter of seeds. Cover them using a layer of plastic wrap.

11. Repeat with the rest of the fixings, cutting each one into eight pieces.

12. Serve it with a portion of ginger slices, wasabi, and soy sauce as desired.

13. Special Cooking Tip: The rice mixture can be prepared and stored for up to two hours ahead of dinner time. (Store it unchilled - room temperature, covered with a damp towel. Don't place it in the fridge.)

14. Note: ** Find the sheets in the International Foods section of your store.

Mongolian Beef

Servings Provided: 4
Total Prep & Cook Time: 30 Minutes

Ingredients:

- Flank steak (1 lb.)
- Vegetable oil (.5 cup)
- Cornstarch (.25 cup)
- Green onions (2)

  The Sauce:
- Packed brown sugar (.5 cup)
- Reduced-sodium soy sauce (.25 cup)
- Cloves of garlic (3)
- Fresh ginger (2 tsp.)
- Vegetable oil (2 tsp.)

Preparation Directions:

1. Thinly slice the steak across the grain. Mince the garlic and thinly slice the onions. Grate the ginger.
2. Whisk the soy sauce, garlic, ginger, two teaspoons of vegetable oil, brown sugar, and ¼ cup of water in a medium mixing container. Cook the soy sauce mixture in a medium saucepan until slightly

thickened, about five to ten minutes, and set it aside.

3. Combine the flank steak and cornstarch in a large mixing container.
4. Heat ½ cup of vegetable oil in a large saucepan. Toss the beef into the pan and fry until browned and cooked thoroughly (approx. one to two min.). Line a platter with paper towels. Dump the beef onto the paper to remove any excess of oil.
5. Place the beef and soy sauce mixture into the saucepan using the medium temperature setting, and cook it until the sauce thickens (approximately two to three minutes).
6. Stir in green onions. Serve immediately.

Side - Snack Options

Crab Wontons

Servings Provided: 12 wontons
Total Prep & Cook Time: 35-40 Minutes

Ingredients:

- White crabmeat (6 oz. can)
- Unchilled cream cheese (4 oz.)
- Light mayonnaise (2 tsp.)
- Sriracha sauce (.5 tsp.)
- Bell pepper - any color (2 tsp.)
- Chives (2 tsp. + more for the garnish)
- Freshly cracked black pepper (as desired)
- Wonton wrappers (12)
- Also Needed: 12-count mini-muffin tray

Preparation Directions:

1. Warm the oven to 350° Fahrenheit. Spray the muffin tray with a spritz of cooking oil spray.
2. Mince the chives and bell peppers. Drain and chop the crabmeat. Combine with the mayonnaise,

cream cheese, bell pepper, chives, Sriracha, and pepper.

3. Place one wonton wrapper in each of the muffin cups. You may need to tuck the edges slightly to fit the cup.

4. Fill the center of each wonton cup with crab mixture.

5. Bake the wontons for 15 to 20 minutes. Once the edges are lightly browned, top it off using more chives as desired.

Fried Rice

Servings Provided: 2
Total Prep & Cook Time: ½ hour

Ingredients:

- Jasmine rice (1 cup)
- Chicken broth/water (1.75 cups)
- Sesame oil (3 tsp.)
- Eggs (2)
- Shoestring carrots (.33 cup)
- Frozen peas (.33 cup)
- Sliced green onion (.25 cup)
- Fresh bean sprouts (.33 cup)
- Soy sauce (3 tbsp.)
- Ground mustard (.5 tsp.)
- Ginger (.5 tsp)
- Garlic (1 tsp.)
- Molasses (2 tsp.)

Preparation Directions:

1. Warm the chicken broth/water in a saucepan. Once it starts boiling, toss the rice into the pan and lower the temperature setting to cook until the water is absorbed (15 min.). The finished rice should be fluffy.
2. Whisk the molasses, garlic, ginger, mustard, and soy sauce.
3. When the rice is ready, set the pan aside off of the burner.
4. Prepare a stir fry pan on the heat with one teaspoon of the sesame seed oil.
5. Crack the eggs into the pan and scramble them. Mince the ginger and garlic.
6. Pour in the remainder of the oil and toss in the green onion, carrots, bean sprouts, and peas to stir fry for three to four minutes.
7. Pour in the rest of the oil (1 tsp.) and rice. Stir fry it for three to four minutes. Toss in the soy sauce mixture and continue cooking an additional three to four minutes.
8. Serve with a garnish of green onions.

Spicy Green Beans - Keto-Friendly

Servings Provided: 4
Total Prep & Cook Time: 15 Minutes

Ingredients:

- Fine sea salt (1 tsp.)
- Green beans (1 lb.)
- Dark soy sauce (1 tbsp.)
- Fresh ginger (2 tbsp.)
- Garlic (2 cloves)
- Rice vinegar (1 tbsp.)
- Black pepper (1 tsp.)
- Sugar (2 tsp.)
- Water (1 tbsp.)
- The Garnish: Sesame seeds
- Optional Ingredient: Red pepper flakes (.5 tsp.)

Preparation Directions:

1. Fill a large frying pan half full of water and wait for it to heat at a low simmer.
2. Trim the green beans and add to cook about three to four minutes until they're tender.
3. Dump the beans into a colander, rinsing with cold water. Drain and set them aside for now.

4. Mince the ginger and garlic. Whisk the rest of the fixings in a bowl.
5. Use the med-low temperature setting to warm the sauce, stirring for three minutes or until heated. Toss it over the beans and serve with a sprinkle of sesame seeds.
6. Note: This recipe offers 9g net carbs, 2g protein, and 52 calories.

Dessert

Deep & Dark Ganache Cake

Servings Provided: One 2-layered cake/varies/approx. 24 servings
Total Prep & Cook Time: 1 ¼ Hours + chill time

Ingredients:

- Chopped bittersweet chocolate (6 oz.)
- Hot brewed coffee (1.5 cups)
- Large eggs (4)
- Sugar (3 cups)
- Canola oil (.75 cup)
- Vanilla extract (2 tsp.)
- A-P flour (2.5 cups)
- Salt (1.25 tsp.)
- Baking cocoa (1 cup)
- Bicarbonate of soda (2 tsp.)
- Baking powder (.75 tsp.)
- Buttermilk (1.5 cups)
- The Frosting:
- Chopped bittersweet chocolate (16 oz.)
- Heavy whipping cream (2 cups)
- Light corn syrup (5 tsp.)

- Also Needed: Square baking pans (8-inches each)

Preparation Directions:

1. Warm the oven at 325° Fahrenheit.
2. Prepare the pans with greased parchment baking paper.
3. Add the chocolate to a container and add the hot coffee. Whisk until it's smooth and slightly cool it.
4. Blend the eggs (high-speed) until mixed and stir in the vanilla, sugar, oil, and mixture of chocolate.
5. Sift the dry fixings (baking powder and soda, salt, cocoa, and flour).
6. Alternately, mix it with the buttermilk and mixture of chocolate, mixing after each addition.
7. Dump it into the pans.
8. Bake it for 30 to 35 minutes. Cool it about ten minutes in the pans before transferring them to wire racks to finish cooling (10 min.).
9. Remove them from the pans and cool thoroughly.
10. Combine the ganache in a large mixing container.
11. Add the cream and corn syrup to a saucepan. Once boiling, pour it over the chocolate and whisk until smooth.
12. Let it rest to cool and thicken for about 45 minutes (room temp). Stir it occasionally. Arrange the first layer of the cake on a serving platter and spread on about 1/3 cup of the ganache. Continue with the layers and top it off over the top.

Chapter 6

Panda Express™ Favorites

Breakfast

Spring Roll

Servings Provided: 15 rolls
Total Prep & Cook Time: 40 Minutes

Ingredients:

- Spring roll wraps (1 Pkg./15)
- Bean sprout (1 lb.)
- Mushrooms (5)
- Carrot (1)
- Lean pork or your choice of protein (4 oz.)
- For Frying: Vegetable oil (1 tbsp./as needed)
- Salt and pepper (1 pinch)

Preparation Directions:

1. Cut the filling ingredients into thin strips.
2. Warm oil in a large skillet.
3. Use the med-high temperature setting to cook the filling components, salt, and pepper, often stirring until cooked thoroughly.

4. Remove the filling ingredients from heat and set aside to cool.
5. Once the filling is cool, arrange a small portion diagonally in between the middle of the wrapper and one corner, as shown in the photo. Roll the wrap over the ingredients to secure the filling.
6. Fold the left and right side of the wrap into the filling and continue to roll the wrapper to the top corner.
7. Dab a bit of water to the tip of the corner to prevent the roll from spilling open when it is fried.
8. Warm a pot of oil until bubbles appear. Make sure you have enough oil that will cover the entire spring roll.
9. Deep fry the spring rolls in med-high heat until golden. Depending on how big your pot is, you can deep fry a few at a time.
10. Once fried, arrange the rolls onto a platter lined with paper towels to absorb the oils before serving.
11. Enjoy every morsel, and save the tip!

Sweet Fire Chicken Breast

Servings Provided: 4
Total Prep & Cook Time: 30 Minutes

Ingredients:

- Pineapple chunks (8 oz. can DOLE™)
- Cornstarch - divided (2 tbsp + 1 tsp.)
- Ground ginger (.25 tsp.)
- Chicken broth (1.5 cups)
- Soy sauce (1 tbsp.)
- Molasses (1 tbsp.)
- Brown sugar (3 tbsp.)
- A-P flour (.5 cup)
- Salt (.25 tsp.)
- Black pepper (⅛ tsp.)
- Paprika (.25 tsp.)
- Garlic salt (.25 tsp.)
- Chicken breast (.75 lb.)
- Chopped carrots (3 medium)
- Canola oil - divided (5 tbsp.)
- Coarsely chopped green pepper (1 small)
- Sliced onion (1 small)
- Hot cooked rice - as desired

Preparation Directions:

1. Drain the pineapple and set it aside for now. Reserve the juice.
2. Mix the cornstarch, pineapple juice, and ginger until creamy.
3. Stir in the molasses, broth, soy sauce, and brown sugar.
4. Combine the flour and seasonings in a large zipper-type baggie. Dice the chicken into one-inch cubes and add them to the bag to toss and coat.
5. Warm a cast-iron skillet using the medium temperature setting to warm four tablespoons of oil. Add the chicken to stir-fry until it's done (not pink inside). Transfer it to a platter and discard the cooking juices.
6. Stir-fry the veggies in the rest of the oil until they're crisp-tender. Mix in the cornstarch mixture and add to the pan. Once boiling, stir for one to two minutes or until the sauce is thickened.
7. Toss the chicken back into the pan with the reserved pineapple to reheat.
8. Serve the delicious chicken with a portion of rice.

Lunch

Hot & Sour Soup

Servings Provided: 2 quarts/6 servings
Total Prep & Cook Time: 45-50 Minutes

Ingredients:

- Pork tenderloin (.75 lb.)
- Olive oil (1 tbsp.)
- Sliced mushrooms (.5 lb.)
- Soy sauce (.25 cup)
- Chicken broth (6 cups)
- Chili garlic sauce (2 tbsp.)
- Black pepper (.75 tsp.)
- Extra-firm tofu (14 oz. pkg.)
- Drained bamboo shoots (8 oz. can)
- Cornstarch (.33 cup)
- White vinegar (.5 cup)
- Sesame oil (2 tsp.)
- Water (.33 cup - cold)
- Green onions (sliced)
- Water chestnuts (8 oz. can)

Preparation Directions:

1. Slice the pork into 1.25-inch by 0.25-inch strips. Drain and cut the tofu into ¼-inch cubes. Drain and slice the water chestnuts.
2. Prepare a Dutch oven with oil and brown the pork until no longer pink. Transfer it from the pan and cover it to keep it warm.
3. Slice and add the mushrooms sautéing until they are tender. Set aside and keep them warm.
4. Add the chili garlic sauce, soy sauce, broth, and pepper to the pan. Wait for it to boil and lower the temperature setting. Put the top on the pot and simmer it for about ten minutes. Toss the meat and mushrooms back to the dutch oven. Stir in the water chestnuts, bamboo shoots, tofu, and vinegar. Simmer it with the lid off of the pot for about ten minutes.
5. Whisk the cornstarch and water until smooth, and slowly stir it into the soup. Wait for it to boil and continue cooking until it is thickened or about two minutes. Transfer the pan from the hot burner.
6. Pour in and mix in the sesame oil. Garnish each of the servings with onions.

Pot Sticker Soup - Slow-Cooked

Servings Provided: 6
Total Prep & Cook Time: 5 ½ Hours

Ingredients:

- Chinese/Napa cabbage (.5 lb.)
- Celery (2 ribs)
- Matchstick carrots (2 medium)
- Green onions (.33 cup)
- Rice vinegar (2 tbsp.)
- Sesame oil (.5 tsp.)
- Soy sauce (2-3 tbsp.)
- Ginger root (2 tsp.) or Ground ginger (.5 tsp.)
- Cloves of garlic (3)
- Reduced-sodium chicken broth (6 cups)
- Frozen chicken potstickers (16 oz. pkg.)
- Optional: Crispy chow mein noodles
- Also Suggested: Four-quart slow cooker

Preparation Directions:

1. Thinly slice the cabbage, green onions, and celery. Mince the ginger root and garlic.
2. Add the first group of fixings into the cooker. Pour in the broth.

3. Set the timer and cook using the low setting until the veggies are tender (five to six hours).
4. Add the potstickers and cook, covered, on high until heated thoroughly, 15-20 minutes.
5. If desired, sprinkle with chow mein noodles before serving. It is also suggested as part of another unique recipe in the cookbook.

Dinner

Chow Mein

Servings Provided: 10
Total Prep & Cook Time: 25 Minutes

Ingredients:

The Sauce:
- Soy sauce (.5 cup)
- Hoisin sauce (1 tbsp.)
- Cooking wine (2 tbsp.)
- Sugar (.25 cup)
- Oyster sauce (2 tbsp.)
- Garlic (1 clove)
- Fresh ginger (2 tsp.)
- Green onions (2 tbsp.)
- Sesame oil (.25 tsp.)

The Chow Mein:
- Lo mein noodles (14 oz.) or Yakisoa dry noodles prepared without the seasoning packs (2 pkg.)
- Vegetable/olive oil - for cooking (2 tbsp.)
- Sliced Napa cabbage (2 cups)
- Sliced white onion (1 large)

- Celery stalks (3 - sliced diagonally into .25-inch slices)

Preparation Directions:

1. Mince the garlic, ginger, and onions.
2. Whisk the sauce ingredients and set it aside for now.
3. Prepare the noodles and drain them in a colander.
4. Warm the oil in a wok/large skillet (med-high temperature).
5. Toss in the celery and onions to cook until the onions are translucent.
6. Stir in the cabbage, sautéing for about one minute (3-4 min.).
7. Stir in the noodles with ½ cup of sauce (2 min.). Serve right away for the best results.

Orange Chicken

Servings Provided: 4
Total Prep & Cook Time: 40 Minutes

Ingredients:

- Soy sauce (3 tbsp.)
- Brown sugar (1 cup)
- Orange juice concentrate (.25 cup)
- Apple cider vinegar (3 tbsp.)
- Diced - boneless chicken breasts (2)
- Eggs (3)
- Red pepper flakes (.5 tsp.)
- Cornstarch (1.5 cups)
- Salt (.75 tsp.)
- Freshly cracked black pepper (.5 tsp.)
- For Frying: Vegetable oil (2 cups) & Coconut oil (1 cup)
- Also Needed: 9x9-inch baking dish

Preparation Directions:

1. Warm the oven to reach 425° Fahrenheit.
2. Whisk the soy sauce, concentrated juice, vinegar, red pepper flakes, and sugar in a saucepan until the fixings are boiling. Set it aside for now.

3. Heat both types of oil in a large wok/skillet using the medium temperature setting.
4. Whisk the eggs in a large mixing container.
5. In another container, whisk the cornstarch, salt, and pepper. Dredge the pieces of chicken through the egg mixture, then in the cornstarch.
6. Cook the chicken pieces until done and transfer them into the baking dish.
7. Drizzle the sauce over the chicken.
8. Bake it for 15 to 20 minutes (toss at 5-minute intervals).
9. Serve with a dish of delicious rice.

Side Dish

Sticky Sesame Cauliflower

Servings Provided: 3-4
Total Prep & Cook Time: 25 Minutes

Ingredients:

- Cauliflower (1 small head/6.5 cups florets)
- Soy sauce - low-sodium/Liquid Aminos for keto (.33 cup)
- Pure maple syrup/agave/honey (.25 cup)
- Minced garlic (1 tbsp.)
- Powdered ginger (.5 tsp.)
- Cornstarch or arrowroot (1.5 tbsp.)
- Rice vinegar (.25 cup)
- Water (.25 cup)
- Toasted sesame oil (1.5 tsp.)
- For the Garnish: Sesame seeds and scallions

Preparation Directions:

1. Set the oven temperature at 450° Fahrenheit. Line the baking tray with a layer of parchment baking paper or mist with some cooking oil spray. Chop

the cauliflower into florets, slicing one side so it will lay flat in the pan. Place them, not touching in the lined prepared pan.

2. Bake them for approximately ten minutes using the center oven rack.
3. In the meantime, whisk the sweetener, ginger, sesame oil, vinegar, soy sauce, and garlic in a medium-sized saucepan.
4. Once it's boiling, whisk in the cornstarch and water until the cornstarch dissolves. Lower the temperature setting to medium, and simmer the mixture for two minutes, continuously stirring until thickened.
5. Flip the florets and bake ten more minutes.
6. Transfer the baking tray to the uppermost rack of the oven to broil for one to two minutes.
7. Serve the florets and sauce with a garnish of scallions and sesame seeds.

Sweet & Sour Sauce

Servings Provided: 8
Total Prep & Cook Time: 10 Minutes

Ingredients:

- White vinegar (.5 cup)
- Water (divided (1.25 cups)
- Sugar (1 cup)
- Cornstarch (.25 cup)
- Red food coloring (2-3 drops for the unique glow)

Preparation Directions:

1. Prepare a saucepan with the vinegar, one cup of the water, and sugar.
2. Whisk the remainder of the water with the cornstarch in a mixing dish.
3. Once it's boiling, add in the slurry, whisking well to simmer for 5 to 7 minutes.

Dessert

Delicious Fortune Cookies

Servings Provided: 10 cookies
Total Prep & Cook Time: 50 Minutes

Ingredients:

- Softened butter (3 tbsp.)
- Sugar (3 tbsp.)
- Vanilla extract (.5 tsp.)
- Egg white (from 1 large egg)
- All-purpose flour (.33 cup)

Preparation Directions:

1. Warm the oven at 400° Fahrenheit. Take a few minutes to write a different fortune on small strips of paper (just like at the restaurant). Prepare a baking tray using a layer of parchment baking paper.
2. Beat the egg white, sugar, butter, and vanilla.
3. Fold in the flour. Spread one tablespoon of batter over each circle. Bake them for four to five minutes - until lightly browned.

4. Place them onto the countertop and cover one cookie with a kitchen towel. Put a fortune in the center of the other cookie; loosen the cookie from the paper. Fold and hold the cookie in half over the fortune strip, so the edges meet for two to three seconds.
5. Arrange the center of the cookie over the rim of a glass and press the ends down to bend the cookie in the middle. Let it cool for one minute before transferring it to a wire rack.
6. Continue the process with each cookie.
7. Note: Pop the cookie into the oven for one minute if it gets too chilled to fold.

Chapter 7

Red Lobster™ Favorites

Breakfast

Cheddar Bay Biscuits

Servings Provided: 14
Total Prep & Cook Time: 20-25 Minutes

Ingredients:

- Granulated sugar (1 tbsp.)
- All-purpose flour (2 cups)
- Kosher salt (.5 tsp. + .25 tsp.)
- Baking powder (1 tbsp.)
- Garlic powder (1 tbsp.)
- Melted unsalted butter - divided (1 stick/8 tbsp. + 4 tbsp./half stick)
- Whole milk (1 cup)
- Mild cheddar cheese (8 oz. shredded)

Preparation Directions:

1. Heat the oven at 400° Fahrenheit. Cover a baking tray using a sheet of parchment baking paper.
2. Sift the garlic powder, ½ teaspoon of salt, flour, baking powder, and sugar into a hefty-sized mixing container.

3. Melt one stick of butter with the milk and cheddar cheese - *don't over mix*.
4. Drop 14 biscuits onto the prepared baking sheet. Bake until the biscuits are browned (10-12 min.).
5. Mix the remaining butter, salt, and parsley to brush the tops of the biscuits before serving.

Crab-Stuffed Mushrooms

Servings Provided: 6
Total Prep & Cook Time: 25-30 Minutes

Ingredients:

- White mushrooms (1 lb.)
- Celery (.25 cup)
- Onion (2 tbsp.)
- Red bell pepper (2 tbsp.)
- Crab claw meat (.5 lb.)
- Shredded cheddar cheese (.5 cup)
- Crushed oyster crackers (2 cups)
- Salt & freshly cracked black pepper (.25 tsp. each)
- Old Bay Seasoning (.5 tsp.)
- Garlic powder (.25 tsp.)
- Egg (1)
- White cheddar cheese (6 slices)

Preparation Directions:

1. Warm the oven at 400° Fahrenheit.
2. Finely chop and sauté the onions, celery, and peppers for two minutes. Place in a bowl and chill in the fridge.

3. Rinse the mushrooms and remove the stems (discard half of them). Combine them with the veggies, chopped stems (if desired), rest of the fixings, except for the cheese slices.
4. Place the mushrooms into baking dishes. Spoon one teaspoon of the mixture into each cup and sprinkle with cheese to bake.
5. Bake them until lightly browned (12-15 min.).

Shrimp Quiche

Servings Provided: 4-6
Total Prep & Cook Time: ½ Hour

Ingredients:

- Pre-baked pie crust (1 - 9-inch)
- Petite Alaskan shrimp (4 oz.)
- Gruyere cheese (2/3 cup grated)
- Whisked eggs (2)
- Light sour cream (1 cup)
- Green onions/chives (1 tbsp.)
- Black pepper and salt (as desired)

Preparation Directions:

1. Devein, cook, and peel the shrimp.
2. Warm the oven to 350° Fahrenheit.
3. Sprinkle the shrimp over the pie crust, adding the grated cheese.
4. Finely chop the chives or onions. Combine the eggs, pepper, salt, sour cream, and green onions.
5. Slowly pour the mixture into the pie crust.
6. Bake for 25 to 30 minutes. Serve warm or chilled.

Sparkling Fruit For Brunch

Servings Provided: 2
Total Prep & Cook Time: 2 ¼ Hours

Ingredients:

- Fresh fruit of choice (2 servings)
- Sugar (.5 cup)
- White wine/champagne (1 cup)
- Freshly chopped mint (.5 tsp.)

Preparation Directions:

1. Choose from melon balls, strawberries (hulled & sliced lengthwise, pears, peaches, pears, or nectarines(seeded, peeled, and quartered). Combine the fruit gently in a container with the sugar.
2. Mix and pour the chosen beverage to almost cover the fruit.
3. Pop it into the fridge to chill for one to two hours.
4. Enjoy in a chilled champagne glass with a friend on a lazy day! It's worth the wait!

Lunch

Clam (& Potato) Chowder

Servings Provided: 6
Total Prep & Cook Time: 45 Minutes

Ingredients:

- Minced clams (2 each - 6.5 oz. cans)
- Crispy bacon (2 strips)
- Medium onion (1)
- All-purpose flour (2 tbsp.)
- Potatoes (4 medium/1.75 lb.)
- Water (1 cup)
- Dried savory (.25 tsp.)
- Salt (.5 tsp.)
- Black pepper (.125 tsp.)
- Dried thyme (.25-.5 tsp.)
- 2% milk (2 cups)
- Freshly minced parsley (2 tbsp.)

Preparation Directions:

1. Drain the clams, reserving the juice.

2. Fry the bacon in a skillet using the medium temperature setting. Stir it occasionally until it's done and crispy. Transfer the cooked bacon to drain on a layer of parchment paper or paper towels. Break it apart into bits.
3. Chop and add the onion to the drippings. Simmer and stir them until tender or for four to six minutes. Mix in the flour, thoroughly stirring until it's blended. Slowly stir in water and the reserved clam juice. Continue cooking while stirring until it's bubbly.
4. Peel, slice, and add potatoes and seasonings, bringing it to a boil, stirring often. Lower the temperature setting and continue cooking, covered with a lid on the pot until the potatoes are tender - occasionally stirring (20 to 25 min.).
5. Pour in the milk, parsley, and clams to heat thoroughly. Top with bacon and serve.

Crab Alfredo

Servings Provided: 4
Total Prep & Cook Time: 25 Minutes

Ingredients:

- Kosher salt
- Butter (3 tbsp.)
- Fettuccine or linguine (12 oz.)
- Garlic cloves (3 minced)
- A-Purpose flour (3 tbsp.)
- Chicken broth (1 cup)
- Heavy cream (1 cup)
- Old Bay (1 tbsp. + more for sprinkling)
- Freshly grated parmesan (1.5 cups + more for the garnish)
- Black pepper
- Fresh parsley (2 tbsp. + more for garnish)
- Lump crab meat (1 lb.)
- Juice of 1/2 lemon

Preparation Directions:

1. Prepare a soup pot of salted water. Add the noodles and cook until they're *al dente*. Toss them into a colander to drain and toss back into the pot.

2. Add the butter to a frying pan using the medium heat setting.
3. Mince and add the garlic to sauté for about a minute. Sift and mix in the flour lightly browned.
4. Pour the heavy cream and chicken broth into the pot and cook it slowly until it's thickened.
5. Add the parmesan, Old Bay, salt, and pepper, and let melt for about two minutes. Fold in the parsley and crabmeat, tossing until coated. Lastly, add the linguine and stir it well.
6. Garnish with chopped parsley, parmesan, Old Bay, and a squeeze of lemon.

Easy Garlic Shrimp Scampi - Keto-Friendly

Servings Provided: 4
Total Prep & Cook Time: 25 Minutes

Ingredients:

- Jumbo shrimp (1 lb.)
- McCormick's Montreal Chicken Seasoning (1 tsp.)
- Black pepper & salt (as desired)
- Olive oil (1 tsp.)
- Garlic clove (3)
- Butter - microwaved for 15 seconds to soften (3 tbsp.)
- Lemon juice (half of 1 lemon)
- Low-sugar dry white wine - ex. Pinot Grigio (1 cup) Or vegetable/chicken broth (1 cup)
- Optional: Red pepper flakes (1 tsp.)
- Freshly grated parmesan cheese (.25 cup)
- Italian seasoning (1 tsp.)
- For the Garnish: Chopped parsley

Preparation Directions:

1. Peel and devein the shrimp. Give it a good shake of salt, pepper, and chicken seasoning to your liking.

168

2. Add the oil and warm a skillet using the med-high temperature setting.
3. Toss the shrimp into the pan for three to four minutes. Once it turns pink, set it aside for now.
4. Mince and toss in the garlic to sauté until it is fragrant (1-2 min.).
5. Add and simmer the lemon juice, wine, Italian Seasoning, and pepper flakes (1-2 min.). Set to low for two more minutes.
6. Add the butter to the skillet and toss the shrimp back into the pan. Simmer for one to two minutes, and serve using parsley and parmesan cheese.

Shrimp Gazpacho

Servings Provided: 4-6
Total Prep & Cook Time: 2 Hours – Varies

Ingredients:

- V-8 vegetable/tomato/bloody mary mix (20 oz.)
- Olive oil (1 tbsp.)
- Worcestershire sauce (.5 tsp.)
- Red wine vinegar (2 tbsp.)
- Fresh cilantro & parsley (1 tsp. each)
- Tabasco sauce (.25 tsp.)
- Lime juice (1 tbsp.)
- Fresh tomatoes (1 cup)
- Seeded cucumber (.5 cup)
- Celery (.25 cup)
- Green onions (.25 cup)
- Bell pepper (.25 cup)
- Salt and black pepper (to your liking)
- Freshly cooked shrimp (1 cup)
- To Serve: Lime (1 in wedges)

Preparation Directions:

1. Devein and cook the shrimp. Pop it in the fridge to chill.

2. Prep the veggies. Chop the cilantro and parsley. Slice the onions and into ¼-inch pieces. Dice the bell pepper, cucumber, tomatoes, and celery into ¼-inch chunks.
3. Combine all of the fixings (omit the shrimp). Chill it for two hours.
4. Portion into serving dishes and top with two tablespoons of shrimp and a wedge of lime.

Shrimp Kabobs

Total Prep & Cook Time: 15-20 Minutes
Servings Provided: 8

Ingredients:

- Uncooked shrimp (32 medium/1 lb. -peeled & deveined)
- Olive oil (3 tbsp.)
- Crushed garlic (3 cloves)
- Dry bread crumbs (.5 cup)
- Seafood seasoning (.5 tsp.)
- Seafood cocktail sauce (as desired)
- Also Needed: Metal or wooden skewers

Preparation Directions:

1. In a shallow mixing container, mix the oil and garlic. Wait for 30 minutes for the flavors to blend.
2. In another mixing container, combine the breadcrumbs and seafood seasoning.
3. Dredge the shrimp through the oil mixture, then coat it using the crumb mixture.
4. Thread the shrimp onto the skewers.

5. Grill the kabobs with the top on the cooker, using medium heat for two to three minutes or until the shrimp turns light pink.
6. Serve with seafood sauce.

Shrimp Slaw

Servings Provided: 6-8
Total Prep & Cook Time: 60-65 Minutes

Ingredients:

- Green/white cabbage (3 cups)
- Celery (1 cup)
- Spinach (1.5 cups)
- Petite Alaskan shrimp (8 oz.)

  The Dressing:
- Fresh ginger (.5 tsp.)
- Freshly cracked black pepper (.5 tsp.)
- Salt (1 tsp.)
- White wine vinegar (.25 cup)
- Honey (2 tbsp.)
- Mayonnaise (.5 cup)

Preparation Directions:

1. Shred the cabbage and spinach. Thinly slice the celery. Grate the ginger. Devein, cook, and peel the shrimp.
2. Toss the fixings in a large salad container.

3. Prepare the dressing and spritz the salad thoroughly. Save leftover dressing for a side dish.
4. Chill the salad for at least one hour

Dinner

Ginger - Soy Salmon

Servings Provided: 4
Total Prep & Cook Time: 15 Minutes

Ingredients:

- Honey (3 tbsp.)
- Dijon-style mustard (1 tsp.)
- Soy sauce (.25 cup)
- Sriracha hot chili sauce/another hot sauce (.25 tsp.)
- Grated ginger (.5 tsp.)
- Canola oil (2 tsp.)
- Salmon fillets (4 - 6 oz. each)
- Black pepper & Kosher salt (as desired)
- Optional - The Garnish: Sliced scallions

Preparation Directions:

1. Set the oven at 400° Fahrenheit
2. Whisk the honey, soy sauce, ginger, mustard, and Sriracha.

3. Warm the oil in an oven-safe skillet using the med-high temperature setting.
4. Dust the salmon with pepper and salt before adding to the skillet.
5. Once the pan is hot, arrange the salmon in the pan and cook for two to three minutes (unmoved to form a crusty layer).
6. At that point, turn them over and place them into the heated oven. Bake them for five to six minutes, leaving the middle slightly pink. Remove and place on the platter to serve.
7. Pour the drippings from the skillet and warm the pan on the stove using the medium-high temperature setting.
8. Dump the soy sauce mixture into the pan and simmer for two to three minutes until thickened.
9. Pour the glaze over the salmon. Top it off with scallions as desired.

Parrot Isle Coconut Shrimp

Servings Provided: 6
Total Prep & Cook Time: 35-40 Minutes

Ingredients:

- Uncooked jumbo shrimp (1.5 lb.)
- Shredded - sweetened coconut (1.5 cups)
- Panko breadcrumbs (.5 cup)
- Egg whites (4 large)
- Louisiana-style hot sauce (3 dashes)
- Black pepper and salt (.25 tsp. each)
- All-purpose flour (.5 cup)

  The Sauce:
- Cider vinegar (1 tsp.)
- Apricot preserves (1 cup)
- Crushed red pepper flakes (.25 tsp.

Preparation Directions:

1. Warm the oven to reach 425° Fahrenheit. Put a wire rack onto two baking trays, coating the racks using a spritz of cooking oil spray. Peel and remove the veins from the shrimp, leaving the tails intact.

2. Use a shallow bowl and toss the coconut with the breadcrumbs, removing half of the mixture to use later.
3. In another dish, whisk the egg whites, salt, pepper, and hot sauce.
4. Sift the flour in another container.
5. Dip the shrimp in flour to cover lightly, shaking off any excess batter.
6. Dip them in the egg white mixture and coconut mixture.
7. Arrange the shrimp on the racks of the prepared pans. Bake them until the coconut is lightly browned and shrimp turns pink or for five to six minutes per side.
8. While they are cooking, mix the sauce components in a saucepan. Cook and stir them using the med-low temperature setting until the preserves are melted.
9. Serve the shrimp with sauce.

Roasted Maine Lobster Bake

Servings Provided: 6
Total Prep & Cook Time: 55 Minutes

Ingredients:

- Fresh/frozen-thawed lobster tails (6 tails / 4-5 oz. each)
- Finely chopped shallots (3 tbsp.)
- Olive oil (3 tbsp.)
- Jalapeno pepper (1 seeded)
- Garlic cloves (3 minced)
- Whole plum tomatoes - undrained (28 oz. can)
- Julienned soft sun-dried tomatoes - not packed in oil (.5 cup)
- Sugar (1 tsp.)
- Dry red wine (.5 cup)
- Italian herb seasoning (2 tsp.)
- Optional: Smoked paprika (.5 tsp.)
- Salt (.25 tsp.)
- Pepper (.125 tsp.)
- Red wine vinegar (1 tbsp.)
- Butter (2 tbsp.)
- To Serve: Hot cooked linguine and minced fresh parsley

Preparation Directions:

1. Cut through the bottom of the lobster tail - lengthwise down the center using a heavy-duty pair of kitchen scissors.
2. Place the lobster tail, cut side up, onto a cutting block. Slice through the lobster meat and shell. Pick the healthy meat from the shell and dice it into one-inch pieces. Set the lobster shells aside for now.
3. In a six-quart stockpot, heat oil using the medium-high temperature setting, add the minced jalapeno and cook until tender or for one to two minutes. Mince and add the garlic to sauté for one additional minute.
4. Pour in the dried tomatoes, tomatoes, sugar, seasonings, and wine, breaking up tomatoes with a spoon. Add in the reserved lobster shells. Wait for it to boil. Lower the temperature setting and continue cooking. (Put a top on the pot to cook for about half an hour, occasionally stirring.) Dump the shells into a colander to drain. Mix in the vinegar and set it aside.
5. Warm the butter in a large frying pan using a med-high temperature setting. Finely chop and toss in the shallots to cook, stirring until tender.
6. Add the lobster meat, and cook it for two to four minutes or until the meat is opaque. Stir it into the tomato mixture. Once it starts boiling, lower the heat setting and simmer, uncovered, two to three minutes or until the meat is firm but tender.
7. For Serving: Fill the lobster shells with tomato mixture. Serve with linguine and a dusting of parsley.

Steamed Blue Crab

Servings Provided: Varies - 12 crabs
Total Prep & Cook Time: 30 Minutes

Ingredients:

- Blue male crabs (1 dozen - large)
- Your favorite beer (1 can)
- Minced garlic (1 tbsp.)
- Sliced onion (.25 cup)
- Bay leaves (2)
- Old Bay Seasoning (8 tbsp.)
- White vinegar (.5 cup)
- Cocktail sauce (to your liking)

Preparation Directions:

1. Use a steamer tray in a large stockpot to prepare the crabs.
2. Pour the onion, bay leaves, garlic, beer, vinegar, and two tablespoons of the Old bay into the pot. Wait for it to boil and remove it from the burner.
3. Place the crabs in the steamer tray with the belly-side facing down. Sprinkle with the rest of the seasoning.

4. Cover and steam for 15 minutes using the high-temperature setting.
5. Serve them when ready with cocktail sauce and extra Old Bay as desired!
6. Note: Select the male crabs since they are cleaner and meatier than the females.

Special Tartar Sauce

Servings Provided: 1.5 cups
Total Prep & Cook Time: 5-6 Minutes (+) extra time to chill

Ingredients:

- Onions (3 tbsp.)
- Carrots (1 tbsp.)
- Mayonnaise (1 cup)
- Sweet pickle relish (2 tbsp.)
- Sugar (1 tbsp.)

Preparation Directions:

1. Finely dice the onions and mince the carrots.
2. Combine all of the fixings and mix well.
3. Refrigerate at least two hours, preferably overnight.

Dessert

Lava Cake

Servings Provided: 6
Total Prep & Cook Time: 40 Minutes + overnight chill

Ingredients:

- Chocolate chips (6 oz.)
- Butter - cut into pats (10 tbsp.)
- Sugar (.5 cup)
- Flour (.5 cup)
- Cocoa powder (3 tbsp.)
- Baking powder (.75 tsp.)
- Eggs (3)
- Also Needed: Custard cups (6)

Preparation Directions:

1. Lightly spray the custard cups.
2. Warm a saucepan (med-low) to melt the chocolate chips. Stir until creamy and add the butter - slowly - until melted.

3. Stir in and melt the sugar. Pour it into a container for now.
4. Sift the baking powder, flour, and cocoa powder into the chocolate using a hand mixer. Toss in each of the eggs, continuously stirring until mixed using the medium beater setting.
5. Dump the mixture into the cups. Cover using a layer of plastic wrap and pop in the freezer overnight.
6. Warm the oven at 375° Fahrenheit. Discard the plastic and bake them for 15-18 minutes. The center will still be moist and the edges firm.
7. Cool for about five minutes and invert them onto a serving platter to serve warm.

Triple Berry Sangria

Servings Provided: 1 Large Pitcher
Total Prep & Cook Time: 30 Minutes To Chill

Ingredients:

- Fresh berries: Strawberries - Blueberries & Raspberries (1 cup of each)
- Fresh ginger (1 teaspoon-sized knob)
- Berry-flavored juice - ex. Ocean Spray (1.5 cups)
- Berry-flavored vodka - ex. Absolut raspberry (1.5 cups)
- Sugar (.5 cup/as desired)
- Red wine - ex. Barefoot Merlot (750 ml bottle)
- Ginger ale (1-2 cups)
- Ice cubes (as needed)
- To Garnish: Mint sprigs

Preparation Directions:

1. Remove the hull from the strawberries. Peel and mash the ginger.
2. Prepare a super-sized pitcher, and add all three berries, vodka, ginger, fruit juice, and sugar. Mix well.

3. Cover the pitcher and let the berries blend their flavors in the refrigerator for about half an hour. Remove the piece of ginger.
4. Right before it's time to serve, stir in the wine, ginger ale, and ice cubes.

Chapter 8

Panera Bread™ Favorites

Breakfast

Cinnamon Crunch Bagel

Servings Provided: Varies
Total Prep & Cook Time: 2 Hours - 2 overnight – Varies

Ingredients:

- Active dry yeast (1 tsp.)
- Sugar - divided (2.5 tbsp.)
- Salt (2.5 tsp.)
- Warm water (1 cup)
- Flour (3.5 cups)
- Salted butter (3 tbsp.)
- Brown sugar (.25 cup)
- Granulated sugar (.25 cup)
- Ground cinnamon (1 tbsp.)
- Baking soda (1 tbsp.)

Preparation Directions:

1. Whisk the water, yeast, one tablespoon sugar, and 1.5 teaspoons salt, and let it sit for ten minutes.

2. Mix in the flour using an electric mixer and dough hook or knead the dough by hand for five minutes. (The dough will be sticky.)
3. Let the dough rest for 10 to 12 minutes and knead again for three additional minutes.
4. Toss it into a mixing bowl and wait for at least four hours or refrigerate overnight.
5. Shape the bagels by pulling the dough apart and shaping it into a thick snake-like shape. Attach two ends together and place them onto an oiled parchment paper-lined baking sheet. Let the dough sit for an hour.
6. Combine granulated sugar, brown sugar, and cinnamon and set aside.
7. Melt the butter in a microwave-safe dish.
8. Warm the oven to 500° Fahrenheit after the bagels have set.
9. Prepare a big pot of water. Once it's boiling, add one tablespoon baking soda, 1.5 tablespoons of granulated sugar, and one teaspoon of salt.
10. Using tongs, place the bagels into the pot for one minute per side.
11. Set them back onto an oiled baking tray, brush with butter, and top with the sugar mixture.
12. Bake for 18-20 minutes, and cool to serve.

Spinach & Cheese Egg Souffle

Servings Provided: 4
Total Prep & Cook Time: 35 Minutes

Ingredients:

- Butter-flake crescent rolls - ex. Pillsbury (8 oz. tube)
- Milk (2 tbsp.)
- Large eggs - divided (5 + 1 for brushing)
- Heavy cream (2 tbsp.)
- Monterey Jack cheese (.25 cup)
- Parmesan cheese (1 tbsp.)
- Sharp cheddar cheese (.25 cup)
- Fresh spinach (3 tbsp.)
- Bacon (4 slices)
- Salt (.25 tsp.)
- Asiago cheese (.25 cup)
- Also Needed: Ramekins (4/approx 4.5 inches in diameter)

Preparation Directions:

1. Warm the oven at 375° Fahrenheit. Shred all types of cheese. Fry and crumble the bacon. Finely chop the spinach.

2. Prepare a microwaveable container and mix five of the eggs, heavy cream, milk, bacon, cheddar cheese, parmesan, Monterey jack, salt, and spinach. Microwave it for half of a minute. Stir and cook it using 20-second intervals for about four to five times until thickened - slightly.
3. Unroll the crescent roll dough into four rectangles. Press them together to make a rectangle. Roll out each rectangle until it's a six by six-inch square.
4. Spray the ramekins with a cooking oil spray.
5. Lay a crescent roll in each dish. Dump one-third cup of the egg mixture on top of each one. Sprinkle using the Asiago and fold the crescent roll dough overtop the eggs.
6. Whisk the last egg and in a small dish and lightly brush it over the tops of each of the crescent roll dough.
7. Bake it until browned or about 20 minutes.

Lunch and Soups

Autumn Squash Soup - Vegan

Servings Provided: 6
Total Prep & Cook Time: 35-40 Minutes

Ingredients:

- Large apple (1)
- Butternut squash (4 cups roasted)
- Large yellow onion (half of 1)
- Salt (1 tsp. + more as needed)
- Cinnamon (1-2 pinches)
- Coconut oil (1 tbsp.)
- Curry powder (.5-1 tsp. or to taste)
- Vegetable broth (3.5 cups)
- Almond milk - unsweetened vanilla (.5 cup)

Preparation Directions:

1. Peel, core, and cube the squash and apple. (Honeycrisp is sweeter than the Granny Smith option.) Dice the onion.

2. Cube and prepare the squash with salt and cinnamon. Roast it for 30 minutes at 425° Fahrenheit.
3. In the meantime, prepare a large skillet using the coconut oil (med-high temperature setting). Sauté the apple and onion with a sprinkle of salt and curry powder until the mixture is softened (10 min.).
4. Add the milk, broth, and squash to the rest of the skillet fixings. Wait for it to boil.
5. Reduce the temperature setting and cook (lid off) for 20 minutes, adding salt as desired.
6. Pour the soup into a high-speed blender and pulse until it's creamy.
7. Serve on the side with a grilled cheese sandwich or crusty bread.

Broccoli Cheddar Soup

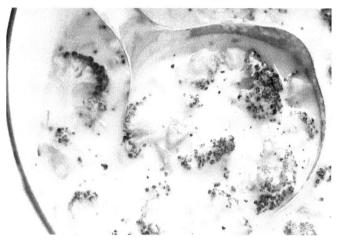

Servings Provided: 4
Total Prep & Cook Time: 45 Minutes

Ingredients:

- High-quality unsalted butter (half of 1 stick)
- Yellow onion (half of 1 medium)
- Garlic (2 cloves)
- Half & Half (2 cups) or (1 cup each milk +heavy cream)
- Chicken broth (3 cups)
- Separated flour (2 tbsp.)
- Nutmeg (.25 tsp.)
- Carrots (.25 cup)
- Broccoli florets (4 cups/about 1 head)
- Sharp cheddar cheese (2.5 cups)
- Salt and pepper (as desired)

Preparation Directions:

1. Prep the fixings before you start the recipe to make it simpler. Mince the garlic and onion. Julienne the carrots, and break the broccoli into florets. Grate the cheese and let it come to room temperature.

2. Prepare a pot to melt the butter using the medium temperature setting. Toss in the onions. Sauté them until softened and translucent (5 min.).
3. Stir in the garlic and sauté them for an additional minute.
4. Fold in one tablespoon of flour and sauté them for about one minute.
5. Slowly pour in the chicken broth and nutmeg.
6. Stir in the Half & Half, raise the heat slightly to thicken the broth for about five minutes.
7. Adjust the temperature setting to medium. Dump the carrots and broccoli into the soup and simmer - occasionally stirring - until the veggies are tender.
8. Extinguish the heat and put the pot on a cool burner. Let the base cool for about five minutes.
9. Sprinkle the rest of the flour (1 tbsp.) over the shredded cheese.
10. Add the cheese/flour in four separate batches, stirring to incorporate as each batch is added.
11. Once the cheese is melted and combined, serve and enjoy it!

Greek Lemon Chicken Orzo Soup - Slow-Cooked

Servings Provided: 4 quarts/12 servings
Total Prep & Cook Time: 4 Hours 50-55 Minutes – Varies

Ingredients:

- Olive oil (2 tbsp.)
- Chicken breasts (2 lb. into ½-inch pieces)
- Reduced-sodium chicken broth (5 - 14.5 oz. each)
- Freshly chopped kale/spinach/Swiss chard (8 cups)
- Carrots (2 large)
- Onion (1 small)
- Lemon zest (4 tsp./1 medium lemon)
- Lemon juice (.25 cup)
- Black pepper (.5 tsp.)
- Cooked brown rice (4 cups)
- Suggested: Six-quart slow cooker

Preparation Directions:

1. Finely chop the onion and carrots. Coarsely chop the kale. Discard the bones and skin from the chicken. Cut and slice the lemon in half and then into wedges.

197

2. Warm one tablespoon of oil in a skillet using the med-high temperature setting.
3. Add half of the chicken into the skillet and fry it until it's browned. Transfer it to the cooker.
4. Finish cooking the chicken and toss it in with the veggies, lemon juice, lemon zest, pepper, and broth.
5. Slow-cook the chicken - covered - using the low setting until it is tender (4-5 hours).
6. Stir in the rice, heating thoroughly and serve.

Summer Corn Chowder

Servings Provided: 6
Total Prep & Cook Time: 40 Minutes

Ingredients:

- Butter (1 tbsp.)
- Medium onion (1)
- Fresh parsley (1 tbsp.)
- Red potatoes (1 lb./3 medium)
- Green onions (2)
- Fresh/frozen corn (1.5 cups/approx. 7 oz.)
- Chicken broth - Reduced-sodium (3 cups)
- Half & Half cream (1.25 cups - divided)
- Salt (.5 tsp.)
- Freshly cracked black pepper (.25 tsp.)
- All-purpose flour (3 tbsp.)

Preparation Directions:

1. Thinly slice the onions and mince the parsley. Chop/cube the onions and potatoes.
2. Prepare a large saucepan to melt the butter using the med-high temperature setting. Mince and toss in the onion to cook until softened, sautéing them for two to four minutes. Stir in the potatoes, corn,

broth, one cup cream, green onions, pepper, and salt. Wait for the mixture to boil.

3. Lower the temperature setting and simmer, covered, until the potatoes are tender (12-15 min.).

4. Whisk the flour and remaining cream in a small mixing container until it is creamy smooth, and stir it into the soup.

5. Wait for the soup to boil. Mix and stir it for one to two minutes or until slightly thickened. Stir in the parsley.

Salad & Side

Mac & Cheese

Servings Provided: 8
Total Prep & Cook Time: 35 Minutes (see notes)

Ingredients:

- Medium pasta shells/elbow macaroni (1 lb.)
  The Roux:
- Butter (.5 cup)
- Flour (.5 cup)
  The Sauce:
- Shredded Cracker Barrel Vermont (3.5 cups)
- White cheddar (1 block = 2 cups)
- Flour (3 tbsp.)
- Half & Half (2.5 cups)
- Milk - preferably whole (1.5 cups)
  The Seasonings:
- Onion powder (1 tsp.)
- Black pepper & salt (.5 tsp. of each)
- Ground mustard (1 tsp.)
- Hot sauce (1 tbsp.)
- Also Needed: 1 lightly greased 9 by 13-inch casserole dish

Preparation Directions:

1. Shred the cheese (room temp) and set it aside. Sprinkle it with three tablespoons of flour and toss.
2. Boil a pot of water and cook the pasta until it's almost al dente. Dump and drain it in a colander thoroughly when finished.
3. Measure out the sauce fixings—Microwave the milk in three 30-second increments, stirring in between cooking.
4. Melt the butter in a saucepan using the medium temperature setting. Sift and whisk in the flour for one minute. Slowly whisk in the Half & Half and milk. Whisk for about three minutes.
5. Add the seasonings and hot sauce. Adjust the temperature setting to low. Slowly sprinkle and fold in the shredded cheese.
6. Whisk continuously until smooth and thickened. Remove from heat. Add boiled pasta and stir to combine. It's ready to serve.
7. Notes: You can alternately bake the meal. Boil the pasta for one minute less than al dente. Transfer it into the casserole dish. Garnish it with crushed Ritz crackers.
8. Bake it at 325° Fahrenheit for 15 minutes. Wait for about five minutes before serving.

Strawberry Poppyseed Salad

Servings Provided: 10
Total Prep & Cook Time: 30 Minutes

Ingredients:

- Sugar (.25 cup)
- Slivered almonds (.33 cup)
- Romaine lettuce (1 bunch/8 cups)
- Onions (1 small)
- Fresh strawberries (2 cups)
  The Dressing:
- Sugar (2 tbsp.)
- Mayo (.25 cup)
- Sour cream (1 tbsp.)
- 2% milk (1 tbsp.)
- Cider vinegar (2.25 tsp.)
- Poppy seeds (1.5 tsp.)

Preparation Directions:

1. Prep the fixings. Tear the lettuce. Slice the berries into halves and thinly slice the onions.
2. Dump the sugar into a cast-iron skillet. Cook and stir it using the med-low temperature setting until melted and caramel-colored (10 min.). Stir in the

almonds until coated. Smear the mixture onto a layer of foil to cool.

3. Toss the onion, romaine, and strawberries in a large salad serving container. Mix the dressing fixings and toss them in with the salad.

4. Break the candied almonds into pieces and sprinkle over salad. Serve immediately.

Dinner

Green Goddess Cobb Salad With Chicken

Servings Provided: 10
Total Prep & Cook Time: 65-70 Minutes

Ingredients:

- Ripened avocado (1 medium)
- Cucumber (.25 cup)
- Tomatoes (2 medium)
- Falafel Mix (6 oz. pkg.)
- Plain yogurt/sour cream (.5 cup)
- Freshly minced parsley (1 tsp.)
- 2% milk (.25 cup)
- Salt (.25 tsp.)
- Torn romaine lettuce (4 cups)
- Baby spinach (4 cups)
- Large eggs (3 hard-boiled & chopped)
- Bacon (8 crispy and crumbled strips)
- Pitted and chopped Greek olives (.5 cups)
- Crumbled feta cheese (.75 cup)

Preparation Directions:

1. Chop and remove the seeds from the cucumber and tomatoes. Peel and chop the avocado.
2. Prepare the falafel according to package instructions. Once it's cooled enough to handle, crumble or coarsely chop it.
3. Whisk the milk, sour cream, parsley, salt, and cucumber.
4. Toss the romaine and spinach. Add them to a platter, adding the crumbled falafel, and the remainder of the fixings over the greens.
5. Drizzle using dressing and serve.

Soba Noodle Bowl With Edamame

Servings Provided: 5
Total Prep & Cook Time: 35-40 Minutes

Ingredients:

- Water (6 cups)
- Frozen/fresh edamame (14 oz.)
- Rice vinegar (3 tsp.)
- Paprika (.5 tsp.)
- Chili powder (3 tsp.)
- Ground sea salt (2 tsp. or to taste)
- Nutritional yeast (1 tbsp.)
- Harissa or cayenne pepper (.25 tsp./as desired)
- Red miso paste (3 tbsp.)
- Vegetable oil/water (2 tsp.)
- Medium carrots (2)
- Baby portobello mushrooms (2 cups)
- Small white onion (1)
- Baby spinach leaves (1 cup)
- Kale (1 cup)
- Freshly thyme minced (1.5 tsp.)
- Soba noodles (1 bunch)
- Freshly cracked black pepper & sea salt (as desired)
- _Optional_:
- Freshly chopped cilantro

- Lime wedges

Preparation Directions:

1. Heat a pot of water and cook the edamame for five minutes. Rinse and drain in a colander using cold water until it's cool. Dislodge the beans from the pods.
2. Prepare a pot with six cups of water, adding in the vinegar, nutritional yeast, harissa/cayenne, chili powder, paprika, and sea salt. Simmer using low heat.
3. Warm a skillet using the med-high heat setting and add the oil or water.
4. Finely slice the carrots, onions, and mushrooms. Sauté for 5-7 minutes, stirring occasionally.
5. Massage the kale and remove the stems. Coarsely chop it before adding it to the hot pan with the salt, pepper, onions, mushrooms, and carrots.
6. Simmer until the kale begins to wilt. Add the spinach and sauté until the spinach starts to wilt. Extinguish the heat.
7. Raise the heat under the broth, and wait for it to boil. Add the soba noodles. Boil the noodles until tender (3 min.). Remove from the heat and put a ½ cup of the broth into a small mixing container.
8. Mix in the red miso to the ½ cup of reserved broth. Whisk until it's fully incorporated without lumps. Pour and stir the miso mixture back into the pot of broth and noodles.
9. Put the vegetables in a deep bowl. Pour the noodles and broth over the veggies. Add the cilantro, edamame, and a bit of fresh-squeezed lime juice. Serve.

Dessert

Caramel Apple Scones

Servings Provided: 4
Total Prep & Cook Time: 35 Minutes + cool time

Ingredients:

- All-purpose & Whole wheat flour (.5 cup of each)
- Salt (.25 tsp.)
- Baking powder (1.5 tsp.)
- Brown sugar (2 tbsp.)
- Chilled butter (3 tbsp.)
- Half & Half cream (.25 cup + 2 tbsp.)
- Egg yolk (1 large)
- Vanilla extract (1.5 tsp.)
- Apple (peeled & shredded - 2/3 cup)
- Ice cream topping - Caramel (1 tbsp.)

Preparation Directions:

1. Warm the oven in advance to 400° Fahrenheit.

2. Whisk the flours, salt, baking powder, and brown sugar. Blend in the butter until it's coarsely crumbled.
3. Combine and whisk the egg yolk, cream, and vanilla in another bowl. Add it to the dry fixings just until moistened. Peel, shred and mix in the apple. Scoop the mixture onto a floured space on the countertop to knead about ten times.
4. Pat the mixture into a five-inch circle. Slice it into four wedges and arrange them on an ungreased baking tray.
5. Set a timer to bake the scones until they are nicely browned (15 to 20 min.). Cool for about ten minutes. Decorate it using the caramel topping and serve.

Cinnamon Coffee Cake Dessert

Servings Provided: 15-20
Total Prep & Cook Time: 20 Minutes + 1-hour - minimum chill time

Ingredients:

- Unchilled butter (1 cup)
- Unchilled eggs (4 large)
- Vanilla extract (2 tsp.)
- Sugar - divided (2.75 cups)
- A-P flour (3 cups)
- Baking soda (1 tsp.)
- Ground cinnamon (2 tbsp.)
- Salt (1 tsp.)
- Sour cream (2 cups)
- Chopped walnuts (.5 cup)
- Also Needed: 10-inch baking tube

Preparation Directions:

1. Warm the oven at 350° Fahrenheit. Lightly grease the pan.
2. Cream butter and two cups of sugar until smooth. Mix in one egg at a time, mixing thoroughly after each addition. Mix in the vanilla.

3. Combine the salt, flour, and baking soda. Mix alternately with sour cream, mixing to blend.
4. Spoon approximately one-third of the batter into the pan.
5. Mix the nuts, cinnamon, and rest of the sugar. Sprinkle another third over the batter in the pan. Continue with two layers.
6. Bake the cake for 60-65 minutes. Cool for 10 to 15 minutes. Place it onto a wire rack to finish cooling.

Jumbo Blueberry Muffins

Servings Provided: 8
Total Prep & Cook Time: 35 Minutes

Ingredients:

- Unchilled butter (.5 cup)
- Sugar (1 cup)
- Large eggs (2)
- Buttermilk (.5 cup)
- Vanilla extract (1 tsp.)
- A-P flour (2 cups)
- Salt (.25 tsp.)
- Baking powder (2 tsp.)
- Fresh/frozen blueberries (2 cups)
  The Topping:
- Sugar (3 tbsp.)
- Ground cinnamon & nutmeg (⅛ teaspoon of each)

Preparation Instructions:

1. Set the oven temperature at 400° Fahrenheit. Line or grease jumbo muffin cups.

2. Cream the sugar and butter until it's fluffy (5-7 min.). Mix in the eggs, stirring thoroughly after each addition. Stir in the vanilla and buttermilk.
3. In a separate mixing container, sift the salt, baking powder, and flour. Mix it into the creamed mixture and stir until incorporated. Add in the blueberries.
4. Fill the muffin cups 2/3 of the way full. Mix the topping fixings and sprinkle over the tops.
5. Bake the batch for 20 to 25 minutes.
6. Cool them about five minutes before removing from the pan onto a wire rack to slightly cool before serving warm.
7. *For Regular-Sized Muffins*: Prepare the batter and dump it into the *standard* muffin cups. Bake them for 15 to 20 minutes. Yields are about 16 standard muffins.

Pumpkin-Apple Muffins With Streusel Topping

Servings Provided: 1.5 dozen
Total Prep & Cook Time: 50 Minutes + cooling time

Ingredients:

- Pumpkin pie spice (1 tbsp.)
- Sugar (2 cups)
- A-P flour (2.5 cups)
- Salt (.5 tsp.)
- Baking soda (1 tsp.)
- Lightly whisked eggs (2 large
- Vegetable oil (.5 cup)
- Canned pumpkin (1 cup)
- Apples (2 cups)
  The Topping:
- A-P flour (2 tbsp.)
- Sugar (.25 cup)
- Ground cinnamon (.5 tsp.)
- Butter/margarine (1 tbsp.)
- Also Needed (paper-lined muffin cups (18 ct.)

Preparation Directions:

1. Set the oven at 350° Fahrenheit.
2. Whisk/sift the flour, baking soda, sugar, salt, and pumpkin pie spice.
3. Combine the eggs, pumpkin, and oil. Mix them into the dry ones. Finely chop and fold in the apples. Fill the muffin cups ¾ of the way full.
4. Prepare the topping by combining the sugar, flour, and cinnamon. Blend or chop in the butter to form coarse crumbs. Scoop one teaspoon over each muffin.
5. Bake them for 30-35 minutes. Let them cool in the pan for ten minutes before moving them onto a wire rack to completely cool before storing.
6. To freeze, securely wrap them in foil or pop them into individual freezer bags for easy removal later. Be sure to label each package using the date and recipe name for storage - up to three months.
7. When it's time to eat, defrost the muffin (s) at room temperature, or choose an alternate method as directed below:
   a. Pop them into a microwave - unwrapped on a napkin or plate. Microwave on high about half of a minute for each muffin.
   b. For a regular oven, warm the foil-wrapped muffins at 350° Fahrenheit for 10-15 minutes.

Chapter 9

Starbucks™ Favorites

Breakfast

Everything Bagels

Servings Provided: 6 bagels
Total Prep & Cook Time: 30 Minutes

Ingredients:

- Almond flour (2 cups)
- Baking powder (1 tbsp.)
- Onion powder (1 tsp.)
- Italian seasoning - dried (1 tsp.)
- Garlic powder (1 tsp.)
- Divided - large eggs (3)
- Low-moisture shredded mozzarella cheese (3 cups)
- Cream cheese (5 tbsp.)
- Everything Bagel Seasoning (3 tbsp.) Recipe below

Preparation Directions:

1. Set the oven at 425° Fahrenheit. Prepare a rimmed baking tray using a silpat or layer of parchment baking paper.

2. Whisk or sift the flour, baking powder, onion powder, garlic powder, and Italian seasoning until all are combined.
3. Whisk one of the eggs in a bowl.
4. Combine the mozzarella and cream cheese. Microwave them for 1.5 minutes. Stir and microwave one more minute. Mix well.
5. Whisk the last two eggs with the flour until well mixed. Portion the dough into six pieces, rolling them into a ball.
6. Indent the center of each one to make the ring. Stretch it to form the bagel.
7. Brush each of the rings using the egg wash. Top it off with the seasoning.
8. Bake on the center rack for 12 to 14 minutes until they are browned to your liking.

Everything Bagels Seasoning

Servings Provided: 1 cup
Total Prep & Cook Time: 5 Minutes

Ingredients:

- Poppy seeds (3 tbsp. + 1 tsp.)
- Toasted sesame seeds (.25 cup)
- Minced dried onions (3 tbsp. + 1 tsp.)
- Coarse sea salt (2 tbsp.)
- Dried garlic flakes (3 tbsp. + 1 tsp.)

Preparation Directions:

1. Combine each of the fixings and store the seasoning in a closed container.
2. It contains 2.6 grams of net carbs if you're counting.

Lemon Bread

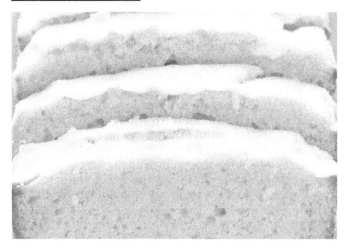

Servings Provided: 15 slices
Total Prep & Cook Time: 1 ¼ Hours

Ingredients:

- Eggs (6)
- Melted - cooled butter (9 tbsp.)
- Unchilled cream cheese (2 tbsp.)
- Vanilla (1 tsp.)
- Heavy whipping cream (2 tbsp.)
- Coconut flour (.5 cup + 2 tbsp.)
- Salt (.5 tsp.)
- Baking powder (1.5 tsp.)
- Monkfruit Classic (.66 cup)
- Fresh lemon juice (4 tsp.)
- Zested lemons (2 - reserve 1 tsp. for the glaze)
  The Glaze:
- Lemon zest (1 tsp.)
- Monkfruit powder (2 tbsp.)
- Lemon juice (2 tsp.)
- Heavy whipping cream (a splash)

Preparation Directions:

1. Set the oven at 325° Fahrenheit and line the bread pan using a layer of parchment baking paper.
2. Melt butter and wait for it to cool.
3. Beat the eggs, heavy whipping cream, salt, cream cheese, monkfruit, vanilla, and baking powder until it's thoroughly combined.
4. Stir in the melted butter, lemon zest, coconut flour, and lemon juice.
5. Dump the batter into the bread pan.
6. Bake it until the top of the bread is just beginning to brown (55-60 min.). Perform a test using a toothpick. Poke it into the center of the cake. The cake's done if it comes out clean.
7. Prepare the glaze. Combine the lemon juice, monkfruit powder, lemon zest, and the heavy whipping cream. Whisk until the glaze is smooth.
8. Pour the glaze over warm bread, spreading it out using a knife or spatula so that it covers the top and drips over the sides.

Pumpkin Bread

Servings Provided: 10
Total Prep & Cook Time: 70 Minutes

Ingredients:

- All-purpose flour (1.5 cups)
- Cardamom (.25 tsp.)
- Nutmeg (.5 tsp.)
- Allspice (.25 tsp.)
- Cinnamon (.5 tsp.)
- Clove (.25 tsp.)
- Salt (.75 tsp.)
- Sugar (1 cup)
- Baking soda (1 tsp.)
- Note: If you use pumpkin spice, use a scant 2 tsp. of the spices mentioned
- Pumpkin puree (1 cup)
- Eggs (2)
- Vegetable oil (.5 cup)
- Roasted & salted pumpkin seeds (.33 cup)
- Vanilla (.5 tsp.)
- Also Needed: 9 by 5 by 3-inch baking dish

Preparation Directions:

1. Warm the oven in advance to reach 350° Fahrenheit. Lightly spritz the baking dish using a cooking oil spray.
2. Sift or whisk all of the dry fixings in a large mixing container (spices, baking soda, sugar, salt, and flour).
3. In another mixing container, whisk the eggs, oil, puree, and vanilla. Mix the fixings until it's lump-free.
4. Dump the mixture into the baking dish with a sprinkling of pumpkin seeds over the top.
5. Bake it for 50 minutes to one hour until done. Test for doneness using a cake tester or toothpick.
6. Cool the bread for about five minutes in the pan and place it on a cooling rack. It's best to cut the bread when it's cooled.
7. *Special Note*: Don't use olive or peanut oil

Turmeric Latte

Servings Provided: 1
Total Prep & Cook Time: 5 Minutes

Ingredients:

- Unsweetened almond milk (.66 cup)
- Honey (1.5 tsp.)
- Ground turmeric (.75 tsp.)
- Ground cinnamon (.125 + more to garnish)
- Ground ginger (.125 tsp.)
- Optional: Black pepper (.125 tsp.)
- Hot brewed espresso (2 tbsp.)

Preparation Directions:

1. Use a 2-cup glass measuring cup to stir the ginger, cinnamon, turmeric, pepper, almond milk, and honey.
2. Microwave the mixture using the high setting for one minute.
3. Use a milk frother to prepare the mixture until frothy.
4. Place the espresso in a glass and top with the prepared almond milk mixture.
5. Serve with a dusting of cinnamon.

Veggie & Hummus Protein Boxes

Use these combinations just like they do at Starbucks!

One serving each:

#1 Bistro:

Ingredients:
- Dried cranberries (1/8 cup)
- Apple - sliced (half of 1)
- Almonds (1/8 cup)
- O Organics® Honey Graham Cracker (2)
- Cheese (1 oz.)

#2 Bistro:

Ingredients:
- Apple - sliced (half of 1)
- Grapes (10)
- Whole wheat pita (halved - 1)
- Peanut Butter (1 tbsp.)
- Cheese (1 oz.)
- O Organics® Cage-Free Boiled Egg (1)

#3 Bistro:

Ingredients:
- Whole wheat pita (1)
- String cheese (1)
- Cucumber (6 slices)
- Baby carrots (10)
- O Organics® Grape Tomatoes (10)
- O Organics® Traditional Hummus (.25 cup)

Dessert

Cranberry Bliss Bar

Servings Provided: 3 dozen triangle bites
Total Prep & Cook Time: 45-50 Minutes

Ingredients:

- Also Needed: 13x9-inch pan
- Cubed butter (.75 cup)
- Unchilled large eggs (2)
- Light brown sugar - tightly packed (1.5 cups)
- Vanilla extract (.75 tsp.)
- A-P flour (2.25 cups)
- Salt (.25 tsp.)
- Baking powder (1.5 tsp.)
- Cinnamon (.125 tsp.)
- Dried cranberries (.5 cup)
- Coarsely chopped white baking chocolate (6 oz.)
  The Frosting:
- Unchilled cream cheese (8 oz. pkg.)
- Confectioner's sugar (1 cup)
- Melted white baking chocolate (6 oz.)
- Chopped dried cranberries (.5 cup)
- Optional: Grated orange zest (1 tbsp.)

Preparation Directions:

1. Set the oven to reach 350° Fahrenheit.
2. Melt the butter in a microwave-safe container, mixing in the brown sugar. Cool the mixture slightly.
3. Mix in one egg at a time, and stir in the vanilla.
4. In another container, whisk the baking powder, salt, flour, and cinnamon. Shake it into the butter mixture. Fold in the cranberries and chopped chocolate. Spread the thick batter into a greased baking pan.
5. Bake it until it's nicely browned (18 to 21 min.), but don't overbake. Cool it on a wire rack.
6. Prepare the frosting. Mix the confectioners' sugar, cream cheese, and orange zest until smooth. Gradually mix in ½ of the melted white chocolate, spreading it over the blondies.
7. Sprinkle with cranberries and drizzle with the remaining melted chocolate.
8. Cut it into triangles. Place them in a container in the fridge.

Eggnog Latte

Servings Provided: 2.5 Quarts
Total Prep & Cook Time: 10 Minutes

Ingredients:

- Eggnog (4 cups)
- Chocolate milk (5 cups)
- Heavy whipping cream - divided (1 cup)
- Instant coffee granules (2 tbsp.)
- Rum extract (1 tsp.)
- Vanilla extract (2.5 tsp.)

Preparation Directions:

1. Combine ½ cup of the cream, the milk, eggnog, and coffee granules in a saucepan. Heat it thoroughly.
2. Transfer the pan onto a cool burner, and mix in the extracts.
3. Beat the rest of the cream until stiff peaks form. Dollop it over the eggnog and serve.

Peppermint Mocha

Servings Provided: 1
Total Prep & Cook Time: 20 Minutes

Ingredients:

The Syrup:
- Mint leaves (30)
- White sugar (.75 cup)
- Water (.75 cup)
- Cocoa powder - Special dark (.5 cup)

The Peppermint Mocha:
- Chocolate-mint syrup (3 tbsp.)
- Warm milk (.33 cup)
- Strong coffee (6 oz.)
- Optional: Whipped cream & Sprinkles

Preparation Directions:

1. Rinse the leaves and pat them dry. Rip them into small pieces and combine with the cocoa powder, water, and sugar.
2. Boil for about 10 minutes and let the syrup cool.
3. Strain the syrup using a mesh strainer into a plastic container or jar.
4. It will remain okay to drink for about two weeks stored in the fridge.

Pumpkin Scones - Vegan & Gluten-Free

Servings Provided: 8
Total Prep & Cook Time: 45-50 Minutes

Ingredients:

- Unchilled pureed cooked pumpkin (1.25 cups)
- Coconut oil (.5 cup)
- Unchilled maple syrup (.75 cup)
- Coconut butter - manna (.25 cup)
- Hot water (.25 cup)
- Salt (1 dash)
- Cloves (.5 tsp.)
- Cinnamon (1 tsp.)
- Allspice (.25 tsp.)
- Nutmeg (.125 tsp.)
- Tapioca starch (1 cup)
- Coconut flour (1.5 cups)
- Pure vanilla extract (1 tbsp.)

Preparation Directions:

1. Pour the coconut oil and butter into a glass container or another oven-safe baking dish. Pop it into the microwave to heat.

2. Blend the mixture with the hot water, maple syrup, vanilla, pumpkin puree, and spices into a large mixing bowl, mixing until it's a smooth mixture using an immersion blender.
3. Add the tapioca starch and coconut flour to the liquid mixture using a wooden spoon to incorporate the fixings. Knead the dough into a large ball.
4. Cover a cutting board with a layer of parchment baking paper. Add the dough ball and flatten into a 1-inch tall mound.
5. Divide it into eight triangles. (Don't separate the scones yet.) Pop it into the fridge for 20 minutes.
6. Warm the oven to reach 350° Fahrenheit.
7. Once the scones have chilled, slowly spread the scones apart.
8. Bake them for 22 to 26 minutes. Put them on a cooling rack for about ten minutes.
9. Toss the glazing fixings into a blender using the high setting until creamy smooth.
10. Cool it slightly, drizzle the glaze over each scone, and *reserve* about 1/3 of the mixture (leaving it in the blender).
11. Measure and add in the pumpkin spice drizzle fixings into the blender. Mix it using the high setting until it's creamy. Scoop it into a piping bag or squeeze bottle and decorate the scones.
12. Serve the scones warm or chilled.
13. Note: If using homemade pureed cooked pumpkin, make sure it is strained well.

Chapter 10

Boston Market™ Favorites

Breakfast & Brunch

Honey Baked Ham

Servings Provided: 8-10
Total Prep & Cook Time: Minutes

Ingredients:

- Whole cloves (1 tsp.)
- Smoked pork picnic shoulder (7 lb. - bone-in or out)
- Sugar (2 cups)
- Brown sugar - packed or honey(1 cup)
- Thawed - frozen orange juice concentrate (6 oz.can)

Preparation Directions:

1. Use a sharp knife to make crosswise slits (½-inch apart).
2. Put the ham in a container with sugar and water to soak for at least two days in the fridge.
3. Dump the water and arrange the ham in a roasting pan. Pour honey and orange juice over the meat and pop in the cloves.

4. Wrap the ham tightly with foil and set the oven at 200° Fahrenheit for six to seven hours until done. Baste it occasionally with the honey mixture.
5. Remove the foil for the last 15 minutes to bake at 450° Fahrenheit if you prefer a crispier skin.

Cranberry Sauce

Servings Provided: Varies
Total Prep & Cook Time: 10 Minutes

Ingredients:

- Smucker's Simply Fruit Orange Marmalade 1 (10 oz. jar)
- Jellied cranberry sauce (16 oz. can)
- Ground ginger (.25 tsp.)
- Finely chopped walnuts (1/3 cup)
- Fresh cranberries - sliced (2 cups)
- Also Needed: 2-quart saucepan

Preparation Directions:

1. Warm the saucepan using the med-low temperature setting. Use a rubber spoon to stir the marmalade, jellied sauce, and ginger until combined and melted (6-8 min.).
2. Fold in the sliced cranberries (low heat), stirring frequently.
3. Continue cooking the cranberries (not mushy - but not too crunchy either).
4. Fold in the nuts. Refrigerate with a plastic cover when cooled. Enjoy them for a week or so.

Lunch

Chicken Pot Pie

Servings Provided: 6
Total Prep & Cook Time: ½ Hour

Ingredients:

- Canola oil (2 tbsp.)
- Medium onion (1)
- A-P flour (.5 cup)
- Poultry seasoning (1 tsp.)
- Chicken broth (14.5 oz. can)
- 2% milk (.75 cup)
- Cooked cubed chicken (3 cups)
- Frozen mixed veggies - thawed (10 oz./about 2 cups)
- Refrigerated pie crust (1 sheet)

Preparation Directions:

1. Set the oven to warm at 450° Fahrenheit. Warm the oil in a large pan using the med-high temperature setting.

2. Chop the onion and sauté it in the pan until tender. Mix in the poultry seasoning and flour. Slowly, whisk in the milk and broth.
3. Boil and stir until thickened (2-3 min.). Add the veggies and chicken.
4. Transfer to a greased nine-inch deep-dish pie plate, adding the crust over the filling: Flute the edges and slice slits in the crust.
5. Bake the pie in the hot oven (15-20 min.). Yummy!

Tijuana Tortilla Salad

Total Prep & Cook Time: 15 Minutes
Servings Provided: 4-6

Ingredients:

- Iceberg lettuce - finely sliced - washed & spun dry (half of 1 head)
- Medium tomato (1 - cored and diced)
- Shredded cheddar cheese (1 cup)
- Cilantro (2 sprigs)
- Beef Chili with Beans (1 cup)
- Tortilla chips (12)
- Optional: Jalapeños

    Additional Toppings:
- Salsa
- Corn
- Black beans
- Avocado

Preparation Directions:

1. Rinse the lettuce and cilantro. Remove the leaves from the cilantro. Tear the lettuce and mix with the fresh cilantro in a large mixing container. Toss in

the onions, jalapenos, olives, tomatoes, sour cream, and olives around the lettuce.
2. Warm the chili in the microwave about 45 seconds until it's heated.
3. Pour the hot chili in the center of the salad with a dusting of the cheese on top. Scoop a portion of sour cream in the center.
4. Serve it with tortilla chips and other toppings as desired.

Tortellini Salad

Servings Provided: 6
Total Prep & Cook Time: 2-3 hours to overnight - as desired

Ingredients:

- (Cheese tortellini (18-20 oz. pkg.)
  The Dressing:
- Caesar dressing (.75 cup)
- Mayonnaise (.5 cup)
- Diced red bell pepper (.5 cup)
- White wine vinegar (.25 cup)
- Water (3 tbsp.)
- Light dry Caesar Dressing mix (1 envelope)
- Seasoned salt (1 tsp.)
- Salt (as desired)

Preparation Directions:

1. Cook the tortellini according to its package instructions and drain in a colander.
2. In another mixing bowl, combine the dressing fixings. Stir in the tortellini.
3. Chill for several hours or overnight for the best results

Dinner

Baby Back Ribs - Slow-Cooked

Servings Provided: 4
Total Prep & Cook Time: 7 Hours

Ingredients:

- Baby back ribs (2.5 lb./8 pieces)
- Water (5 cups)
- Medium onion (1)
- Celery (2 ribs)
- Garlic - divided (2 tsp.)
- Whole peppercorns - divided (1 tsp.)
- BBQ sauce (.5 cup)
- Plum sauce (.25 cup)
- Hot pepper sauce (1 dash)
- Also Needed: Five-quart slow cooker

Preparation Directions:

1. Slice the onion, mince the garlic, and cut the ribs in half. Toss the ribs into the cooker. Pour in the water, onion, celery, one teaspoon of garlic, and the

peppercorns. Securely close the lid and set the timer for six hours on the low setting.

2. Whisk and heat the bbq sauce, hot pepper sauce, plum sauce, and remaining garlic in a saucepan. Simmer using the medium temperature setting for five minutes or until it's hot. Remove the ribs. Discard cooking juices and veggies.
3. Moisten a paper towel with oil and lightly coat the grill rack.
4. Brush ribs with sauce. Grill, covered, using the med-low temperature setting for eight to ten minutes, turning and basting as needed with the rest of the sauce.

Savory Rubbed Roasted Chicken

Servings Provided: 12
Total Prep & Cook Time: 1.5 Hours + wait time

Ingredients:

- Salt (1 tsp.)
- Paprika (2 tsp.)
- White pepper (1 tsp.)
- Dried thyme (1 tsp.)
- Cayenne pepper (1 tsp.)
- Black pepper (.5 tsp.)
- Onion powder (1 tsp.)
- Garlic powder (.75 tsp.)
- Roasting chicken (6-7 lb.)
- Large onion (1 in wedges)

Preparation Directions:

1. Warm the oven at 350° Fahrenheit. Mix the first eight fixings in a mixing container.
2. Pat the chicken dry using paper towels and arrange it (breast side up) on a rack in a roasting pan. Rub it thoroughly using the seasoning mixture, adding the onion inside the cavity.

3. Tuck the wings under the chicken and use kitchen twine to securely tie the drumsticks.
4. Roast it for 2 to 2.5 hours (Internal temperature of 170° to 175° Fahrenheit). Transfer the cooked chicken to the countertop and tent with foil. Wait for about 15 minutes before slicing it to serve.

Side Dish

Creamed Spinach

Total Prep & Cook Time: 30 Minutes
Servings Provided: 6

Ingredients:

- Water (.25 cup)
- Butter (5 tbsp.)
- A-P flour (.25 cup)
- Half & Half cream (1 cup)
- Salt (as desired)
- Cream cheese (4 oz.)
- Onion (2 tbsp.)
- Garlic (1 tbsp.)
- Black pepper (.5 tsp.)
- Nutmeg (.25 tsp.)
- Frozen & thawed spinach (20 oz.)
- Parmesan cheese (.25 cup - grated)

Preparation Directions:

1. Warm three tablespoons of the butter in a medium-sized saucepan. Once it is hot, sift in the flour and sauté until lightly golden.
2. Slowly pour in the cream, stirring continuously to remove all of the lumps.
3. Then add the cream cheese, stirring until it's all smooth. Set aside - off of the burner.
4. Mince and sauté the onion and garlic in another pan using the remaining 2 tbsp. of butter for 2-3 minutes until it becomes pink or soft.
5. Add the water and spinach to simmer for 8 to 10 min.
6. Mix in the cream cheese sauce and parmesan cheese to the spinach and toss before serving.

Loaded Mashed Potatoes

Total Prep & Cook Time: ½ Hour
Servings Provided: 4-6

Ingredients:

- Small baking potatoes (7)
- Butter (2 tbsp.)
- Milk or cream, more or less depending on the dryness and size of your potatoes (.5 cup)
- Salt (.5 tsp.)
- Chives (1.5 tbsp.)
- Sour cream (.33 cup)
- Bacon (6-8 slices - reserving 2 tbsp. for topping)
- Grated cheddar cheese (.5 cup - reserving 2 tbsp. for the garnish)

Preparation Directions:

1. Cook the bacon until it's crispy before cooling and crumbling. Peel, boil, and mash the potatoes with butter, salt - creaming until fluffy.
2. Add cream to your liking to achieve the desired consistency.
3. Stir in the chives, sour cream, bacon, and grated cheddar cheese.
4. Top with cheese and bacon, and serve at once.

5. You can also leave off the toppings and refrigerate until ready to use.
6. Microwave until warm or heat slowly, covered with foil in a 325° Fahrenheit oven. Add the toppings and serve.

Dessert

Blue-Ribbon Apple Pie

Servings Provided: 8
Total Prep & Cook Time: 1.75 to 2 Hours

Ingredients:

- Pastry Crust (9-inch for double-crust pie)
- *Walnut Layer*:
- Ground walnuts (.75 cup)
- Brown sugar (2 tbsp.)
- Lightly whisked egg (2 tbsp.)
- Melted butter (1 tbsp.)
- 2% milk (1 tbsp.)
- Lemon juice (.25 tsp.)
- Vanilla extract (.25 tsp.)
  The Filling:
- Sliced tart apples (6 cups/4-5 medium)
- Lemon juice (2 tsp.)
- Vanilla extract (.5 tsp.)
- A-P flour (3 tbsp.)
- Cinnamon (1.25 tsp.)
- Ground nutmeg (.25 tsp.)
- Salt (⅛ tsp.)

- Cubed butter (3 tbsp.)
- Sugar (.75 cup)
  The Topping:
- 2% milk (1 tsp.)
- Sugar (2 tsp.)

Preparation Directions:

1. Set the oven to reach 375° Fahrenheit.
2. Roll half of the pastry onto a lightly floured surface until it's about a 1/8-inch-thick circle. Place it in a nine-inch pie plate and trim it until it's even with the rim.
3. Mix the walnut layer fixings and dump it into the pastry shell. Refrigerate it for now.
4. Toss the apples, vanilla, and lemon juice. Whisk and add in the sugar, cinnamon, flour, salt, and nutmeg.
5. Pour the filling over the walnut layer, dotting it with butter. Roll the rest of the pastry dough to a circle (1/8-inch thick). Place it over the filling and flute the edge. Brush the top with milk, and a sprinkle of sugar. Cut slits in the pastry.
6. Put the pie on a baking sheet to catch any drippings. Bake it for 55-65 minutes or until the filling is bubbly. Cool on a wire rack.
7. Notes: You can also prepare a pastry for a double 9-inch pie. Combine 2.5 cups of all-purpose flour and ½ teaspoon of salt. Cut in one cup shortening until it crumbles. Slowly, add four to five tablespoons ice water, tossing with a fork until the dough holds together when pressed. Now, you can portion the dough into two balls. Wrap them in plastic wrap to refrigerate for one hour.

Boston Cream Cupcakes - Shortcut

Servings Provided: 20-24 cupcakes
Total Prep & Cook Time: 20 Minutes

Ingredients:

- Yellow cupcakes (from your favorite recipe)
- Prepared vanilla pudding (homemade/boxed - 2 cups)
- Heavy cream (1 cup)
- Vanilla extract (1 tbsp.)
- Semi-sweet chocolate chips/Ghirardelli or another high-quality brand (12 oz. bag)

Preparation Directions:

1. Mix the vanilla and pudding and add it to a decorator's gun with a large enough opening to inject pudding into the cupcakes.
2. Gently poke the gun into the center of each cupcake and inject about one tablespoon of the pudding into the cupcake.
3. Once all cupcakes have been injected, cover and chill them while making the topping.

4. Heat cream in a saucepan using the medium temperature setting - just until the sides start to have tiny bubbles.
5. As soon as it gets to this point, transfer it to a cool burner and add chocolate chips. Whisk until the chips have melted and everything is smooth.
6. Set out a layer of wax paper and grab the slightly chilled cupcakes.
7. Spoon a portion of the topping onto the center of a cupcake, covering the pudding opening, adding more topping around the edges to cover the top of cupcake completely with the topping.
8. Set cupcake onto the paper to cool.
9. Repeat until all cupcakes are covered with the topping, and place into a covered container to chill for at least one hour. (The topping will get firmer but not hard.)
10. You may have a bit of extra topping to use on top of ice cream. Store any extra topping in a covered container in the fridge for up to one week.

The Ultimate Chocolate Brownie

Servings Provided: 8
Total Prep & Cook Time: 1 ¼ Hours

Ingredients:

- Sugar (1 cup)
- Water (.25 cup)
- Brown sugar (.5 cup - packed)
- Cubed butter (2/3 cup)
- Optional: Instant coffee granules (2 tsp.)
- Bittersweet chocolate chips - divided (2.75 cups)
- Unchilled large eggs (4)
- Vanilla extract (2 tsp.)
- A-P flour (1.5 cups)
- Baking soda (.5 tsp.)
- Salt (.5 tsp.)
  Also Needed:
- 9-inch square baking pan
- A layer of parchment baking paper

Preparation Directions:

1. Warm the oven at 325° Fahrenheit, adjusting the rack to the lowest bar.

2. Line the pan with paper with the ends extend up the sides.
3. Combine the butter, sugars, water, and coffee granules in a heavy-duty saucepan. Wait for it to boil, constantly stirring. Remove the pan to a cool burner and add 1 ¾ cups of the chocolate chips. Stir them continuously until melted. Cool the mixture slightly.
4. Whisk the eggs until foamy (3 min.). Add the vanilla and slowly mix in the chocolate mixture.
5. Next, whisk/sift the baking soda, flour, and salt. Mix in the chocolate mixture, adding the rest of the chocolate chips. Dump it into the papered pan.
6. Bake, the mixture for 40-50 minutes, or until a toothpick inserted in the center comes out with moist crumbs (do not overbake). Cool completely in the pan on a wire rack.
7. You will love how easy it is to remove the delicious brownies from the pan. Simply lift them using the outer edges of the parchment baking paper to remove brownies from the pan. Cut them into eight squares.

What Did You Think of Copycat Recipes?

First of all, thank you for purchasing this book, Copycat Recipes: The Ultimate Cookbook on How to Make the Most Delicious & Famous Restaurant Fast Food Dishes at Home. I know you could have picked any number of books to read, but you picked this book and for that I am extremely grateful.

I hope that it added great value and quality to your everyday life. If so, it would be really nice if you could share this book with your friends and family.

If you enjoyed this book and found some benefit in reading this, I'd like to hear from you and hope that you could take some time to post a review on Amazon. Your feedback and support will help me to greatly improve my writing craft for future projects and make this book even better.

I want you to know that your review is very important and so, if you'd like to **leave a review**, all you have to do is go on Amazon and review your order. I wish you all the best in your future success in your virtual meetings!

Thank you and enjoy the recipes!

Emma Dennis

CPSIA information can be obtained
at www.ICGtesting.com
Printed in the USA
BVHW071540090321
602013BV00005B/1094